LIVING FAITH

*An Orthodox Christian Conversation
with Evangelicals*

LAWRENCE R. FARLEY

ANCIENT FAITH PUBLISHING
CHESTERTON, INDIANA

Living Faith: An Orthodox Christian Conversation with Evangelicals
Copyright © 2023 Lawrence R. Farley

Published by:
Ancient Faith Publishing
A Division of Ancient Faith Ministries
1050 Broadway, Suite 6
Chesterton, IN 46304

Unless otherwise noted, Scripture quotations are taken from the New King James Version, © 1979, 1980, 1982 by Thomas Nelson, Inc. Used by permission.

ISBN: 978-1-955890-57-1

Library of Congress Control Number: 2023946827

Printed in the United States of America

Cover design by Samuel Heble

Cover images
Bottom left to right: Photo by City Church CA on Unsplash; St. Nicholas Russian Church in Bucharest, Romania, by Wirestock via iStock; photo by Nagel Photographer via Shutterstock; photo by Ekaterina Polischuk via iStock.
Top left to right: Photo by Javier Cruz Acosta via Shutterstock; icon from the Tretyakov Gallery via Wikimedia Commons; photo by Chris Bradshaw via Shutterstock; photo by Iuliia Zavalishina via iStock.

Dedicated to the memory of Fr. Bill Hewton,
wonderful Evangelical and worthy man of God

Contents

Why Was This Book Written?

This book was not written as an attack on Evangelicals or Evangelicalism but as an attempt to understand and explain Evangelicalism to non-evangelicals (such as the Eastern Orthodox) and also to provide an Orthodox response to the challenges Evangelicals often raise against the teachings of the Orthodox Church. That is, it is intended as a fair, plainspoken, and irenic conversation between Orthodox and Evangelicals.

The presuppositions of both groups are deeply held and rarely examined by those holding them (which is why they are called "*pre*suppositions"). This often leads to unfruitful conversations between the two groups in which neither really understands the other. Because both groups consist of conservative Christians and both groups therefore use the language of Scripture (e.g., the term "born again"), each can imagine that they are talking about the same thing when in fact they are talking about very different things. It is rare that either group begins a conversation by defining their terms, much less taking care to discover what the other group means by the words they use.

Here an example might help. When an Evangelical asks an Orthodox, "Are you saved?" the Evangelical is asking whether the Orthodox has had a saving experience of Christ and has devoted his life to serving the Lord. The Orthodox, on the other hand, interprets the question as meaning, "Have you finished your course and reached perfection, *theosis*, your final goal?" and so of course answers, "No, not yet." Here is not so much disagreement as simple misunderstanding—a misunderstanding that a little explanation of terms and jargon would help to clear up.

It is the same with the issue of Marian devotion. When the Evangelical asks the Orthodox, "Do you worship Mary?" he means, "Do you accord her the same degree of devotion and adoration as you accord to God Himself?" The Orthodox Christian, who of course gives to God alone such divine devotion (traditionally called *latreia* to distinguish it from mere *doulia* or honor), believes the Evangelical is asking whether he loves, honors, and is devoted to Mary. Thus he may answer, "Yes, naturally I worship Mary." Once again, a simple definition of terms would help avoid basic misunderstanding.

This book has as one of its goals the explanation of Evangelicalism for those not familiar with it, and the Orthodox reply to its (sometimes impolite) challenges.

Conversions from Orthodoxy to Evangelicalism and from Evangelicalism to Orthodoxy occur frequently here in North America. The former often consist of merely nominally Orthodox people (usually from ethnic backgrounds, such as Greeks or Russians) who had no real experience of Christ as children. When they come face to face with the living Christ in evangelical churches, naturally they convert and become Evangelicals. They then often denounce Orthodoxy as unchristian and say things like "I used to be Orthodox, but now I am a Christian."

Such people, as well as those who were born into Evangelicalism, naturally tend to equate saving faith in Christ with Evangelicalism. They therefore regard with suspicion all nonevangelical groups, especially those as foreign to their ethos and practice as Orthodoxy. (They often have difficulty differentiating Orthodoxy from Roman Catholicism, especially given that such nonevangelical practices as sacramentalism and Marian devotion are found in both. In these cases, Orthodoxy becomes the dubious benefici-ary of Protestantism's anti-Catholic bias.)

This book is intended to make the case for Orthodoxy to those Evangelicals. As we will see, Evangelicalism is a big tent and con-tains many people of all levels of education. There are many evan-gelical scholars (including those who would prefer to designate themselves as "Reformed" rather than "evangelical"), and like all scholars, they have insights that tend to expand the evangelical world and make generalization even harder than it already is. Unfortunately, given the complexity and magnitude of the task, dialogue with these scholars must remain outside the goals of this volume. This book has a more modest and narrowly focused aim: to respond to the Evangelicals who often visit my humble Orthodox parish and who wonder, since we don't issue altar calls, if we really are born again, if icons are actually idols, why they can't take Communion, and whether we worship Mary. In other words, I am trying to respond to Evangelicals of the pew, not those of the academy.

It is understood that the emotional resistance to Orthodoxy's response will be considerable and perhaps quite visceral. It may be difficult for Evangelicals to put aside their fear that leaving Evangelicalism means leaving real and saving faith in Christ. But fear makes a poor lens through which to view anything. It is the author's hope and prayer that his evangelical brothers and sisters may come to see that Orthodoxy is not the threat to such sav-ing faith they had been led to think, but that both Orthodox and Evangelicals are united in a saving love for the Lord, God, and Savior of all.

Who Are the Evangelicals?

In one sense I have always been and will always be an evangelical, if by that term one means someone devoted to living and sharing the *euaggelion*, the Good News of the eternal life available in Christ.

The problem, of course, with this definition of an evangelical is that it is rather too broad and generous, for it includes pretty much every stripe of Christian of all the major denominations. It includes Baptists such as the late Reverend Dr. Billy Graham, Anglicans such as N. T. Wright, Presbyterians such as Dr. Carl Trueman, Roman Catholics such as Pope John Paul II, and Orthodox such as Fr. Alexander Schmemann. Being spread so broadly, this definition of an evangelical is useless, since the term thus defined is indistinguishable from Christianity itself. It also makes nonsense out of movements like the one producing the colorful and controversial 1994 document "Evangelicals and Catholics Together," for if Catholics *were* Evangelicals, why would one need a movement to help unite them? Obviously our definition of Evangelicalism must be more closely detailed. It must look not just to etymology ("Evangelicals are those who believe the Good News") but to actual church communities on the ground.

This is where the problems arise in earnest, for Evangelicalism is not a homogenous movement, and generalizations are notoriously problematic. Many people claim to be Evangelicals; some of them vigorously disagree with other Evangelicals. One is tempted to say that the tent containing tent revivals is a big tent indeed. Some Evangelicals are scholarly (such as the Pentecostal professor Denis Lamoureux, Associate Professor of Science and Religion at St. Joseph's College in the University of Alberta), and some are less so (such as televangelist Joel Osteen of the disturbingly megawatt smile). Moreover, some individuals may be recognized as Evangelicals by other Evangelicals, though the denominations of which they are a part would not be so recognized (such as C. S. Lewis and J. I. Packer, both of whom were members of the Church of England).

In this study we will examine not evangelical *individuals* but evangelical *churches*—communities and denominations recognized by all as members of the evangelical family. Given that those churches have developed and evolved greatly in the past decades (sometimes to the point of changing beyond recognition), and also given that there is great diversity among those churches and denominations, some generalizing must be allowed. I am aware that almost every statement could find some Evangelical somewhere raising his hand at the back of the room and protesting, "Our group doesn't believe that!" But since this is a small book and not an encyclopedia, such generalizations must be endured. I will do my best to nuance statements where possible and acknowledge existing diversity of evangelical belief and practice.

To begin: Certain characteristics and teachings are common to all evangelical churches.

The first of these is that evangelical churches are comparatively modern, given that the Christian Church has existed for two millennia. That is, those churches did not exist prior to the sixteenth-century Reformation; in fact, they arose even later than that, within the last several hundred years. The fact that Evangelicals claim some commonality with the early and patristic Church (we have already noted that Christians of all kinds and in all centuries have shared a devotion to the Good News), or that they claim to be restoring biblical teaching that was lost during the years of the early and patristic Church, does not refute this. It remains true that *churches*—not teachers or teaching, but *churches*—containing all the components of modern Evangelicalism did not exist until well after the Reformation. That in itself may not serve to delegitimate Evangelicalism, but it must be admitted as an historical component. Many of the cornerstones of Evangelicalism would have been simply incomprehensible to those in the early and patristic Church and puzzling even to the main teachers of the magisterial Reformation, such as Luther and Calvin. This fact is not always appreciated by Evangelicals themselves, who, knowing little of church history, gratuitously assume that the early Church looked more or less like evangelical churches today. It did not.

Secondly, and flowing from the first point, evangelical churches are all Protestant, since they developed from churches that arose during the Protestant Reformation. This means that the central teachings of the Reformation—not excluding its fundamental and visceral allergy to anything Roman Catholic—are a part of its ecclesiastical DNA. (This accounts for the controversy attending the publication of the 1994 document "Evangelicals and Catholics Together.") Anything that cannot demonstrate its Protestant credentials is dismissed without discussion. Teachings from the early Church (such as baptismal regeneration, Marian devotion, the veneration of relics, and the Real Presence of Christ in the Eucharist) are excluded without further thought. *Of course* such teachings must be wrong—they are Catholic. Because of this tribal anti-Catholic element, these teachings are not given a real hearing or considered as possibilities. Because this approach is so fundamental to Evangelicalism, the bias often goes unnoticed and is not necessarily accompanied by actual hostility to Catholics themselves.

Thirdly, evangelical churches are ecclesiastically independent. The individual congregations might belong to a larger federation or an overseeing body (such as Pentecostal congregations in Canada belonging to the PAOC[1] or Baptist congregations belonging to the Baptist Convention[2]), but in the daily governing of their congregations they are independent. That is, they are solely responsible for the hiring and firing of their clergy and the conduct of the life of the congregation. Their association with other congregations of their denomination is entirely voluntary. This in part accounts for some of the diversity within Evangelicalism: If a group wishes to break away from the parent body and form another denomination for any reason whatsoever, it is free to do so. This also accounts for the bewildering variety of denominations in North America all claiming to be evangelical.

Fourthly, the foundation of Evangelicalism is a commitment to conversion. In most evangelical churches, conversion is seen to consist of a penitent person saying a prayer wherein he commits his life to Christ. This is often referred to as "receiving Christ" or "asking Christ to come into your heart." The prayer in which this commitment is offered is sometimes called "the sinner's prayer," and it is understood that by saying this prayer the sinner becomes immediately born again and has her sins forgiven. Though another Christian may give the (often emotional) invitation to say this prayer and make this commitment, the involvement of another is not required.

Anyone, it is felt, can do this, even on her own, after reading the Bible or a tract of Christian literature. There exists a wide variety of such literature urging the reader to say the prayer and make the commitment. (One example is the tract produced by

---

1   Pentecostal Assemblies of Canada.

2   The group from which the Fellowship of Baptist Churches broke away in 1933.

Campus Crusade for Christ[3] entitled, "Have You Heard of the Four Spiritual Laws?") These tracts invite readers to ask Christ into their hearts and offer a sample prayer for doing this. They then assure readers that after sincerely saying the prayer, they have certainly become born again and forgiven and are thereby made members of the Church, even though they may never have set foot in an actual church congregation. The moment of decision and commitment is not only intensely personal but essentially individualistic. The assembled church itself plays no crucial part in this process of new birth and forgiveness.

This conversion process is the *sine qua non*, the essential element, of evangelical experience, and it constitutes "getting saved." Without it, some Evangelicals doubt the reality of one's professed faith. The story of this moment of conversion constitutes one's "testimony" and in many places functions as one's credentials as a true Evangelical. One need not necessarily be able to date it precisely (groups disagree about the importance of the commitment's "datability"), and emotion accompanying the experience is not necessarily required (though it is desirable). But an inability to attest to such a moment of conversion can place one's status as an Evangelical in jeopardy.

One sees immediately from the necessity of such a moment of conversion that the convert must exercise his or her mind and will to convert—that is, he or she must knowingly and voluntarily "ask Jesus into their heart." Children too young to understand the gospel or too young to sincerely say the prayer and make the commitment are thereby excluded from the experience and the ranks of the "born again."

This serves to privilege not only the place of experience but also the place of the intellect and individual will of the person in evangelical theology. The importance of this privilege, though

---

3   Now going by the name "Cru" to avoid the negative associations of the term "crusades" in the minds of Muslims and others.

often unacknowledged, can hardly be overstressed, especially when it comes to sacraments (as we will see later).

Fifthly, the radical individualism of the foundational conversion experience is carried over into the evangelical understanding of the Church. To be "in Christ" means to have undergone the conversion experience of the new birth. Membership in "the Church" is accomplished automatically and immediately on saying the sinner's prayer. Obviously, this "Church" is not the one on the corner into which the convert has not yet entered but "the church of the firstborn who are registered in heaven" (see Heb. 12:23). In other words, this "Church" does not refer to the actual *ekklesia* or gathering of Christians on Sunday for worship but to one's status as a member of the People of God solely by virtue of having had the new birth experience.

Gathering with other Christians on Sunday morning is deemed important for one's spiritual growth but not essential to becoming born again or to being "in Christ." The original commitment to Christ expressed in saying the sinner's prayer alone is salvific. Attempts to ascribe saving significance to anything else are clearly and emphatically denied.

We see this in such tracts as the aforementioned "Have You Heard of the Four Spiritual Laws?" After assuring the reader that he has become born again by saying the prayer, the tract instructs the convert in "How to Be a Dynamic Believer." It mentions six things: "Go to God in prayer daily; read God's Word daily; obey God moment by moment [details are not specified]; witness for Jesus daily; trust God for every detail of your life; and allow the Holy Spirit to control and empower your daily life and witness" (details also not given).[4]

Note that attendance at church and participation in the sacraments are not among these recommended behaviors. Another

---

4   The initials of these six admonitions spell out the acronym "GROWTH."

paragraph, however, is added on: "The Importance of Fellowship with Other Believers." The rationale given is that "several logs burn brightly together; put one aside on the old hearth and the fire goes out." Church attendance is thus helpful but not essential and certainly not salvific. The purpose of such gatherings is confined to "fellowship"—mutual encouragement and comradery. Once again, not a word is said about sacraments.

Sixthly, most evangelical churches are not built on a sacramental foundation, and in many places the Lord's Supper (strenuously differentiated from the Eucharist of the Roman Catholic and other sacramental churches) is served only periodically, sometimes a mere four times a year. Generalization here becomes difficult, with a number of evangelical churches celebrating the Lord's Supper more frequently and ascribing to it more significance than in previous decades. But for many if not most evangelical churches, the Sunday morning service consists of music, a Scripture reading, a sermon, and some prayer.

In the same way, when baptism is administered, it is understood that the immersion (usually a single immersion, not the triple immersion of the early Church) does not convey anything saving, such as the new birth or the remission of sins. Baptism is rather understood as a public confession and announcement of a faith previously acquired through saying the sinner's prayer and asking Christ into one's heart.

Seventh, we note Evangelicalism's firm commitment to the truth of Holy Scripture, to biblicism. Here there is a spectrum of opinion, with some Evangelicals committed to a more literal interpretation of Scripture consistent with historical fundamentalism, while other Evangelicals show more openness to less literal approaches. All Evangelicals, however, acknowledge Scripture as the supreme authority in the Church, often contrasting it with tradition, creedal formulations, and the views of the Church Fathers. For many if not most Evangelicals, the basic meaning of

Scripture is plain and does not require any further interpretive guide, such as creeds, councils, or other sources of tradition.

This is sometimes conveyed in slogans such as "Back to the Bible!" or "The Bible is my only creed." It is expressed sometimes in evangelical statements of faith, wherein a belief in the Bible is article one, with belief in God as Trinity coming afterward as article two. In this approach to Scripture there is a hostility to the very word *tradition*; it is viewed as a rival and therefore a threat to the sole and supreme authority of Scripture. To any doctrine or practice, this biblicism responds almost reflexively, "What does the Bible say?"

Eighth, we note a consistent emphasis on the Cross as the means of salvation (usually paired and contrasted with "works," meaning an attempt to earn one's salvation and standing with God by moral effort). This emphasis on the Cross is rooted in a conviction that man's main plight and problem is guilt and the debt we owe to God for it but cannot pay. The Cross is viewed as the payment to God and the means of eliminating our guilt. In devotion and hymnography, the Cross usually stands alone—separated from the Resurrection of Christ, which is often considered as of little or no salvific value. The Resurrection is seen merely as vindicating Christ's claims and as proof that the payment of the Cross accomplished our salvation.

Ninth, American Evangelicalism is often tethered to conservative politics, so that many consider that voting Republican is a part of good evangelical faith. From the days of Jerry Falwell and his Moral Majority, Evangelicalism and Republicanism have often gone hand in hand. The evangelical defense of Donald Trump should be understood in this context. There have been exceptions, of course, but Evangelicalism often contains a large dose of political commitment.

Tenth, Evangelicals have a heart for missions and often support missionaries working in foreign countries. It is not unusual to see the promotional photos of missionary families whom Evangelicals support adorning the doors of their refrigerators as a reminder to uphold them in prayer.

Finally, consistent with Evangelicalism's self-understanding as being opposed to the Roman Catholic Church and pre-Reformation Christianity generally, the liturgical praxis of their churches takes care to avoid similarity with the liturgical practices of older sacramental churches. This often begins with a heated denial that they *have* a liturgical praxis at all, since "liturgy" is defined by them as a set service written in a book and recited by clergy and people.

Once again, generalization is hazardous, but most evangelical churches prefer a degree of informality in their worship that sets them apart from the older historic churches, such as the Orthodox, Catholic, and Anglican churches. This may include elements such as the lack of vestments for the clergy, an absence of images, statuary, or decoration in the church interior, and the refusal of "trappings" such as holy water or incense. The issue is not a belief in bareness or austerity of worship, necessarily, but the desire to differentiate themselves from those using (for example) vestments, icons, and incense. In this regard, evangelical churches usually do not observe the calendar of the historical church with its alternating seasons of fasting and feast days, nor do they fast communally (such as in Great Lent). Fasting, if done at all, is left to the individual's discretion. Further, because of monasticism's connection with the historic churches, evangelical churches tend to be suspicious of monasticism as an institution.

More could be said about this vast topic, but these are some of the components characterizing most evangelical churches in North America today.

CHAPTER ONE

"The B-I-B-L-E, yes, that's the book for me!"

The Role of Scripture

The title of this chapter, which examines the role of Scripture, comes from an evangelical children's chorus that goes, "The B-I-B-L-E, yes, that's the book for me! I stand alone on the Word of God, the B-I-B-L-E!" Though it is a mere children's chorus (or perhaps because it is a children's chorus), it offers a succinct view of the Evangelical's approach to Scripture. That is, Scripture functions as *the* book, the sole authority, one that is sufficient to answer all religious questions, one that is clear in its meaning and in need of nothing else to interpret it. The Bible is often read independently from centuries of Church interpretation (i.e., from Tradition), so that one "stands alone" on it as the Word of God, a divine Source contrasted with all other sources, which are the mere words of men. This is what many Evangelicals mean by the term *sola scriptura*. In classic Reformation usage, the slogan meant that Scripture is *above* Tradition, with Tradition and the Fathers still having a voice. In modern Evangelicalism, it usually means "Scripture and *no* Tradition," with Tradition and the Fathers being almost entirely rejected as a source.

It is also understood by Evangelicals that because the Bible is *the* Book, it pronounces on everything needed by the Christian and the Church. That being so, if the Bible does not specifically pronounce on something in a definitive and prescriptive way, that thing therefore must not be very important. The Church is bound to do everything the Bible commands it to do, but if the Bible does not command a particular course of action, the Church is free to do whatever it wishes.[5] Thus, some groups who feel that the Bible does not specifically command the Church to keep Sunday as the prescribed day for gathering to worship believe that they are free, in principle at least, to choose another day of the week for their regular gathering.

The supremacy and sufficiency of the Bible have classically been expressed in the interior architecture of small-to-medium-sized Protestant churches. In pre-Reformation days, the central focus of Christians in church was on the altar table, which stood at the front of the nave. In Reformation churches, that focus was changed so that the pulpit or preaching desk became the central focus, with the small table used occasionally for the Lord's Supper being placed in a subordinate position. This admirably expressed the Protestant conviction that Scripture and the preaching of the Word were paramount in the life of the Church. (In modern large churches that use a stage and employ a praise band, the classical pattern has given way once again.)

The role of Scripture was quite different from this in the early Church. In the first century, of course, the term *the Scriptures* referred only to the Hebrew Scriptures. (What exactly constituted those Scriptures was to remain fluid for some time, with some communities using the books of the so-called Apocrypha as Scripture, while other communities read them but relegated them to a subordinate status.[6]) The Hebrew Scriptures were

---

5   Some Protestant groups take a stricter line and assert that they can only do what is specifically commanded, and unless it is commanded, it is forbidden. This is known as the regulative principle of worship.

6   This topic cannot be examined fully here. A good resource is L. M.

regarded as authoritative because Christ regarded them as such (as did all Jews in the Second Temple period) and because Christians believed that the authors of those Old Testament books were "moved by the Holy Spirit" and thus "spoke from God" (2 Pet. 1:21 RSV). The written product was regarded as "God-breathed" (Greek *theopneustos*; see 2 Tim. 3:16), partaking of His divine authority and having God as its ultimate Author. That is why the Old Testament could prophetically foreshadow Christ and the realities of His Kingdom and Church.

The documents of the New Testament were similarly authoritative[7] but in a different way. Their authority derived from the apostolic authority the apostles had from Christ. That is, the authority of the apostles was not confined to the documents and letters they wrote; it was their personal authority and so was found in their oral instructions, directives, and teaching as well.

This was a different sort of authority from that found in the Old Testament authors. The author of 1–2 Chronicles, for example, had no such personal abiding authority; his authority resided entirely in the books he wrote. After he put down his pen, the words he spoke and the orders he gave had no more authority in Israel than those of any other good and pious man. It was otherwise with the apostles. They were men of authority in the Church, and they expected their directives to be followed, precisely because they were the apostles and representatives appointed by Christ Himself. They knew Him and had received all the teaching He entrusted to them for His Church. Thus, the one who welcomed an apostle welcomed Christ Himself in his person (Matt. 10:40).

McDonald's *The Biblical Canon* (Hendrickson Publishers, 2007). See also *The Religion of the Apostles* and *Apocrypha* by Fr. Stephen De Young (Ancient Faith Publishing, 2021 and 2023).

7   Thus Peter could pair the writings of Paul with "the rest of the Scriptures" in 2 Peter 3:16.

That is why St. Paul praised the churches when they accepted and obeyed the directives—literally "the traditions" (in the plural; Greek *paradoseis*)—given by him and the other apostles. In 1 Corinthians 11:2, Paul says, "Now I praise you because you remember me in everything and hold firmly to the traditions, just as I delivered them to you." In 2 Thessalonians 2:15, he exhorts his readers, "Stand firm and hold to the traditions [again note the plural] which you were taught, whether by word of mouth or by letter from us."

Here we see that Paul regarded the traditions he delivered "by word of mouth"—the bulk of his instruction—as of equal authority with the traditions he delivered "by letter from us." What mattered to Paul was that the instructions he gave came from him as an apostle. Their mode of delivery, whether oral when he was with them in person or by letter when he was absent, was utterly irrelevant. Oral or written, the instructions of an apostle came with authority.

We note too that the noun *paradosis* (usually translated as "tradition"[8]) has a verb form, *paradidomi* (usually translated as "to deliver"). In both the noun and the verb forms, the notion refers to someone coming alongside (Greek *para*, meaning "beside") and then giving the person something (Greek *didomi*, meaning "to give"), like someone passing a baton in a relay race. So when Paul refers to "delivering" a teaching, in passages such as 1 Corinthians 11:2; 15:3; and 2 Thessalonians 2:15, the notion of tradition is latent there. The concept of tradition is thus central to the New Testament, for it is the mode of delivery of the authoritative teaching of the apostles.

This notion of the fullness of authority of apostolic Tradition— whether transmitted orally or written—remained potent in the

---

8   The NIV shows its Protestant bias by translating *paradosis* as "tradition" in such negative contexts as Mark 7:8, but as "the teachings we passed on to you" in such positive contexts as 2 Thess. 2:15.

apostolic Church. That is why St. Basil (d. 379) could write about the identical authority of both orally transmitted traditions and the writings of the New Testament. In his *On the Holy Spirit*, Basil wrote:

> Concerning the teachings of the Church, whether publicly proclaimed or reserved to members of the household of faith, we have received some from written sources [i.e., the New Testament], while others have been given to us secretly, through apostolic tradition. Both sources have equal force in true religion. No one would deny either source—no one, at any rate, who is even slightly familiar with the ordinances of the Church. If we attacked unwritten customs, claiming them to be of little importance, we would fatally mutilate the Gospel, no matter what our intentions.[9]

As examples of these unwritten customs, St. Basil mentions making the sign of the cross over new converts and praying facing the east. Doubtless other customs included the mode and meaning of baptism and the Eucharist and the Christian understanding and use of the Old Testament.

Thus, in the Orthodox Church, what is authoritative is the apostolic Tradition in its entirety—a Tradition that includes all the teaching the apostles have given to the Church, including the books they wrote (i.e., the New Testament). We do not speak of "Scripture *and* Tradition," as is often done in the West, because we regard Scripture *as a part of Tradition*. As such, New Testament Scripture is entirely authoritative, possessing, along with the Old Testament writings, the authority of the true and reliable Word of God.

This is the mindset and approach of the Fathers, who regarded

---

9   *On the Holy Spirit* (Crestwood, NY: St. Vladimir's Seminary Press, 1980), 98–100.

Scripture as completely authoritative. Scripture's authority, being part of the Church's Tradition, stood apart from and above the opinions of any single individual in the Church. Men may err, but Scripture can never err.

In reading the Scriptures of the New Testament, we must realize that they were never intended to function as a model or a set of Ikea-style instructions telling us how to construct and run the Church. They do not answer all the questions one might ask—questions such as "How should a Christian pray? Which direction does he face when he prays? How and when should he fast? How does one baptize a convert? May infants be baptized? May one pray for the dead? On which day of the week should the church assemble for its weekly worship? What does one do at worship? What were the roles of the clergy?" The letters of St. Paul and the other apostles were occasional documents, provoked by certain challenges and answering certain questions. They were never intended, as in the evangelical *sola scriptura* approach, to provide a comprehensive program for worship.[10]

Moreover, one faces the question of how to interpret Scripture. Unlike Protestantism, Orthodoxy does not regard the Bible as self-interpreting or its meaning as being so plain as not to require interpretation. Clearly the Bible is not self-interpreting and plain, since many intelligent and pious men have disagreed about its basic meaning. That is why there are so many Protestant denominations and why so many theologians quarrel over basic tenets of faith and practice. The Bible is not a single book but a library, and an interpretive lens is required if one is to reduce the library to a set of directives, teachings, and church instructions.

---

10 It is significant and sobering to reflect that if the Corinthian church had not experienced problems at their celebration of the Eucharist, the entire topic of the Eucharist would have found no mention in the epistles, despite it being an important and weekly occurrence at the heart of Christian worship.

Every denomination has such a lens. It may be the agreements of men in centuries past (such as the Westminster Confession or the Augsburg Confession). It may be the collected pronouncements of the popes. It may be the latest fad from recent best-selling evangelical authors. But everyone has a lens through which they read the sacred text, including the Orthodox.

The Orthodox lens is the *consensus patrum*, the consensus of the Fathers. The Church Fathers were a tremendously varied lot, writing in different languages, in many different lands, across many centuries. Naturally they disagreed with each other about many things. But there remains a core consensus, an impressive number of teachings on which all (or almost all) agreed, and it is this consensus that the Orthodox Church regards as authoritative. It is the lens through which the Church reads Scripture, the mechanism through which the apostolic Tradition reaches all in the Church. That is because Orthodox Christians regard this consensus not as a happy coincidence of opinion but as the result of the Fathers retaining the teaching of the apostles.

For example, if all the Fathers regarded the Eucharist as sacrificial and as the true Body and Blood of Christ, that was because their churches received this teaching originally from the apostles and the Fathers received it in their turn. The authority remains that of the apostles; the consensus of the Fathers merely witnessed to the apostolic source of the teaching, since that teaching was universally received.

This does not mean that for the Orthodox Church, biblical commentary is simply a matter of mindlessly repeating what the Fathers have said. The patristic mindset and approach remain definitive, but as new scholarly tools become available, the work of scholarly interpretation continues.

Unlike the situation in some forms of Evangelicalism, Orthodox biblical interpretation is not a solitary and individual project, with the believer poring over the sacred text and coming to his own independent conclusions. Rather, biblical interpretation is a multigenerational project, with readers and scholars learning from each other, even across the centuries. That is why the works of the Fathers feature so prominently in many Orthodox commentaries. Each commentator builds on the work of what others have done, and all are subject to mutual addition and correction. It is the Church as a whole that is the ultimate commentator on the Bible, not any individual author.

Thus, we Orthodox also believe in the B.I.B.L.E. But we receive it as part of the traditions from the apostles.

CHAPTER TWO

"Blessed assurance! Jesus is mine!"

The Nature of Salvation

As mentioned above in the introduction, Evangelicals consider the event of conversion to be fundamental; to be an Evangelical is to "be saved," and when an Evangelical asks someone "Are you saved?" they are asking if the person has undergone this process of conversion. Those who have not undergone such a conversion are considered "not saved"—that is, in supreme danger of damnation should they die unconverted.[11] It is to their credit, therefore, that Evangelicals will go to great lengths to ensure that as many people as possible undergo this conversion experience and avoid damnation.

Also as mentioned above, the usual mechanism of salvation is sincerely and penitently saying a prayer in which one asks Jesus to forgive one's sins, enter one's heart, and give one the gift of the new birth. This prayer is often known as "the sinner's prayer"; it generally forms the culmination of a (sometimes passionate) sermon in which the preacher invites the listener to

---

11 Some Evangelicals have embraced a more agnostic view regarding the fate of the unconverted, and some have opined that all will finally be saved, regardless of whether or not they have undergone conversion to Christianity. But this movement is comparatively new and not a part of historical Evangelicalism.

say the prayer and make a commitment to Christ. Despite the lack of an altar table as an architectural focus, the invitation is referred to as an "altar call," for it sometimes involves those saying the prayer arising from their seats and coming to stand at the front of the church. It is understood that after the prayer has been said, the one saying the prayer has been forgiven his or her sins and born again.

Many Evangelicals (though not all) believe that those thus regenerated cannot fall away from faith but will remain devoted Christians until their life's end. This doctrine, classically called "the perseverance of the saints" in the Reformed tradition, is often called "eternal security." (This is examined at greater length in Appendix A.)

The stakes involved in the giving of such invitations could not be higher, since it is believed that the eternal destiny of the hearers depends on their choice. Accepting the message and saying the sinner's prayer will result in salvation and eternal joy in heaven, while rejecting the message will result in damnation and eternal punishment in hell. Many Evangelicals believe that everyone who has not accepted the message and undergone conversion will be damned, so that damnation becomes the "spiritual default mode" of the human race.[12]

The issue regarding damnation is primarily one of guilt: one is considered guilty and damned unless one has been saved and forgiven. In this system of salvation, each person is born burdened with a debt of guilt and sin. No one can pay the debt, so doom and damnation await each soul. But Christ died on the Cross, the Sinless for the sinful, taking on Himself the debt and burden of guilt; therefore, now, if one will accept Christ and believe that He has paid the debt, one can be saved and forgiven. Note: Here everything depends on the cognitive understanding of this exchange

---

12 This was the position of St. Augustine, whose thought became constitutive for later Western theology.

as well as the personal decision of the person to accept Christ and benefit from the exchange.

This of course does not include those children too young to understand and accept this exchange, since they cannot make the decision necessary to enter into this saving agreement. Nonetheless (and happily), Evangelicals are reluctant to follow the logic that led men such as St. Augustine to conclude that such young children are damned if they die prior to being baptized.

In short, the evangelical view of salvation is *asacramental* (neither needing nor using any sacramental means to accomplish it), *forensic* (focusing on one's legal status as one forgiven rather than condemned), *immediate* (with the saved achieving the status of being forgiven the instant commitment is made), and *individualistic* (needing no other involvement than that of the convert himself).

The Orthodox have a different understanding of salvation.

Firstly, salvation is *sacramental*, for it begins in baptism. When Peter was asked by a stricken crowd on the Day of Pentecost what they should do to be saved, he replied, "Repent and let each of you be baptized in the name of Jesus Christ for the forgiveness of your sins, and you will receive the gift of the Holy Spirit" (Acts 2:38). Note: What was required of the penitent was baptism, and it was in baptism that the convert received the forgiveness of sins and the gift of the Holy Spirit.[13]

The same understanding of baptism as the way of converting to Christ and receiving forgiveness was taught by Saul's teacher, Ananias. He said to the penitent Saul (or Paul), "Why do you delay? Arise and be baptized, and wash away your sins, calling on His name" (Acts 22:16). Note again: In baptism, sins are washed away.

In his letters Paul would teach this doctrine of baptismal

---

13 In the Orthodox Church, the rite of baptism consists of a triple immersion and the anointing with oil, in which the gift of the Holy Spirit is given.

remission and regeneration. He referred to our salvation as our being "cleansed by the washing of water with the Word" (Eph. 5:26) and as "the washing of regeneration and renewing by the Holy Spirit" (Titus 3:5). The word here rendered "washing" is the Greek *loutron*, "a bath"—a clear reference to the baptismal immersions.

Paul understood baptism as the moment when the convert participates in the death and Resurrection of Christ (see Rom. 6:3f). That was why, when asked by the Philippian jailor how one might be saved, he told him to believe on the Lord Jesus—which clearly involved baptism, since that was what happened immediately as a result (Acts 16:30–33).

Given the salvific significance of baptism, one sees why Peter could simply and boldly assert, "Baptism now saves you" (1 Pet. 3:21): the bath was not simply a bath but also the means whereby one made an appeal to God, answering the call for a cleansed conscience and a new life. It is in baptism that one expresses one's commitment to Christ and makes the saving confession of faith. "To believe" means "to be baptized."[14] It is in baptism that one makes the saving confession with the mouth that Jesus is Lord (Rom. 10:9). It is in baptism that one "calls on the name of the Lord" (Rom. 10:13; compare Acts 22:16). The practice of "asking Christ into your heart" non-sacramentally is not found in the New Testament and was unknown in the entire history of the Church until the rise of American Evangelicalism.

Secondly, for the Orthodox, salvation is not merely forensic (involving our legal status) but also *transformative*. When one becomes a Christian in baptism, one is immediately and fully forgiven one's sins and is initiated into a life of constant repentance and ongoing forgiveness. But as well as bestowing forgiveness,

---

14 Compare Ephesians 1:13—the aorist (i.e., once for all) tense is used to describe the act of believing, not the perfect tense, indicating the definitive moment of baptism.

as said above, baptism also affects regeneration, as the convert receives new life from Christ and is born again, beginning a new life as a child of God. The baptized convert is an entirely new creation (2 Cor. 5:17).

Obviously, Evangelicals also believe in the new birth, but they strictly separate *justification* (i.e., forgiveness) from subsequent *sanctification*, ascribing all saving content to the former. For the Orthodox, this partition of justification from sanctification is wrong: the one and indivisible experience of salvation could be described as *washing* (the cleansing of sin and sinfulness), and as *sanctification* (receiving the Holy Spirit so that one becomes holy), and as *justification* (being forgiven). These are not three separate stages or realities that one undergoes serially (e.g., first justified, then sanctified) but three aspects of a single experience—which is how they are described by Paul in 1 Corinthians 6:11.[15]

This transformation is sometimes called theosis, a transformation in which the convert increasingly grows into the likeness of God. As a number of the Fathers taught, "God became man so that man could become God"—obviously not in the sense of ceasing to be a creature and becoming the Creator, but in the sense of partaking in the divine nature insofar as this is possible for creatures to do (see 2 Pet. 1:4). All that Christ is by nature, He shares with us by grace, so that He becomes the firstborn of many brothers (Rom. 8:29): He is the Son of God by nature; we become sons of God by grace. He is holy by nature; we become holy by grace. He is immortal by nature; we become immortal by grace. It is this entire process of theosis/divinization that is our goal; this is what the Orthodox understand by the word *salvation*. Salvation does not consist merely of being forgiven but of finally becoming entirely like Christ, our elder brother and Savior.

---

15 We note the order of their listing, which makes the evangelical notion of "justified, then sanctified" impossible, for Paul lists sanctification before justification.

That is why the Orthodox regard salvation not as an immediate experience fully accomplished at the moment of conversion but as a process, an ongoing journey that extends throughout one's life and into the age to come. Though one is fully forgiven at the moment of conversion/baptism, forgiveness is not the entire goal—theosis is. This transformation takes time and involves our cooperation. That is why St. Paul bids us "work out our salvation with fear and trembling" (Phil. 2:12). It is also why he referred to Christians in 1 Corinthians 1:18 not as "saved" (in the perfect tense) but as those "who are being saved" (in the present tense):[16] we continue to work out and experience salvation throughout our life.

Further, the Orthodox regard salvation as being not individualistic but *ecclesial*. Since forgiveness and regeneration are the gifts received in baptism, obviously the gathered church community is essential, since no one baptizes himself but each is baptized by another.

In fact, the characteristic Pauline phrase "in Christ" refers not primarily to an individual experience but to the fact of one's incorporation into the Church as the Body of Christ. Salvation consists of our incorporation into Christ, our sacramental union with Him, for it is through this union that we share His sonship and status before God. That is why, in 1 Corinthians 12:13, Paul said, "for by one Spirit we were all baptized *into* one body" (Greek *eis en soma*; emphasis mine). The preposition *eis*, "into," expresses this notion of incorporation. The primary reality of our salvation is our participation in the saved and sacramental body of Christ, the family that offers and receives the Eucharist every Sunday.

Moreover, this salvation is not simply ecclesial, rooted as it is in the weekly eucharistic gathering. It is also *cosmic*. The entire world to come is to be regenerated, born again from the ashes of the old age, in which we now live. That is why Christ referred to

---

16 Greek *sozomenois*.

the age to come as "the regeneration" (Greek *paliggenesia*) in Matthew 19:28. The Holy Spirit, the Life-giver, will bring the world to this new birth and new life. Salvation consists of receiving this future life in our hearts in this age, receiving individually now what will one day transform the entire cosmos. Regeneration is a cosmic reality; in Christ, by His Holy Spirit, we receive this reality and power now and are born again in baptism.

This reveals that our salvation consists in receiving not simply forgiveness but also the gift of life, a power that will destroy death and raise us to immortality. The constant Pauline theme is "death through Adam, life through Christ." Note: not simply forgiveness but *life*. Our salvation is a process, one that begins in baptism and finds its consummation on the Last Day, with the resurrection and redemption of our bodies (Rom. 8:23). For the Orthodox, salvation is *past* (given in baptism), *present* (an ongoing experience and journey), and *future* (reaching its goal when we are finally raised from the dead).

CHAPTER THREE

The Woman at the Christmas Crèche

Mary

G iven that Evangelicals regard salvation primarily as a matter of receiving forgiveness so that one is assured of going to
heaven, and given that this gift of forgiveness is entirely accomplished immediately on saying the sinner's prayer, it is not surprising that Evangelicals see little need of a role for Mary the Mother
of Jesus. After they sincerely say the prayer and commit their lives
to Christ, they have everything they will ever need, so what help
could Mary provide? The role of an intercessor is superfluous.

Again we note that an anti-Catholic bias against Marian devotion accompanies such theologizing. Thus, devotion to Mary and
reliance on her prayers are regarded not simply as unnecessary
but as idolatrous, wicked, and sinful. An Evangelical's response
to any Marian devotion is often quite visceral. A favorite verse
used to combat such devotion is 1 Timothy 2:5, which reads, "For
there is one God and one Mediator between God and men, the
Man Christ Jesus." Mary thus cannot function as a mediator
offering prayer for us, since Christ is the only mediator possible.

Mary is usually regarded as a pious woman but no more holy,
close to God, or significant than anyone else. Her presence is tol-
erated at the Christmas crèche, as her terracotta figure (along
with Joseph's) is set alongside that of the baby Jesus as a part of

the Sunday school's Nativity set, and her part in the Christmas story is played by a child at the Christmas pageant. But that is the only visible role allowed her. Any suggestion that she might have an ongoing role in the life of the Christian is greeted with suspicion and hostility. Jesus' picture may be allowed somewhere on the walls of the Sunday school, but her picture, never. By the day after Christmas, she is gone. The notion of prayer to Mary remains deeply inimical to evangelical theology.

Despite the long and bitter Western war between Catholics and Protestants over Mariology, there is no such separate category as Mariology in the Orthodox Church. Rather, Mariology is simply a subcategory of Christology. It is significant that the only official title given Mary by the ecumenical councils—that of Theotokos—was primarily intended as a statement about Christ and the mode of His Incarnation.[17]

Devotion to our Lord's Mother arose naturally and immediately in the Church as Christians, unhampered by a later Protestant suspicion and resistance to such devotion, reflected sympathetically and imaginatively on what it must have meant to Mary to be the Mother of the Incarnate God. That is, they wondered what it must have been like for a young woman of teenage years to give birth to the Messiah, to nurse Him, teach Him, rear Him, comfort Him, and then to watch Him make startling claims to divinity, perform astonishing miracles, die in horror and pain on the Cross, and then rise again. Christians who worshipped Jesus must have wondered what it was like for Mary to have known that the Child she bore and reared was Almighty God, the One

---

17 The point being that Mary gave birth in the flesh to the divine Word Himself, not simply a human being on whom the Word descended. The title Theotokos (sometimes translated "Mother of God") was intended to safeguard the truth that the Incarnation resulted in the union of two natures in a single *hypostasis* or person—a "hypostatic union," not simply (as Nestorius taught) a conjunction of the divine Word with a human being.

through whom the Father made her and all the world. With such reflections, love, wonder, gratitude, and devotion to her would arise naturally and inevitably.

That is why in the mid-second century we can already find a great desire to learn more about her childhood—a desire that produced the document now known to scholars as *The Protoevangelium of James*. It does not matter that pretty much all the material in the document is legendary and of no real historical value in reconstructing her early life. What matters is that the document witnesses to the immense interest in and love for Mary that grew up immediately in the Church and that moved the author to create such a story.

That is also why in the second century we find, independently of each other, two different comparisons of Mary with Eve, coming from the pens of Justin Martyr and Irenaeus.[18] Both wrote that the knot of the virgin Eve's disobedience was loosed by the obedience of the Virgin Mary. Even the North African writer Tertullian, no fervent fan of Marian devotion, wrote that "as Eve believed the serpent, so Mary believed God. The delinquency which [Eve] caused by believing, the other [Mary] by believing effaced."[19]

The important thing to note is that the same theme was found in the works of a number of different authors writing independently of each other, which shows that interest in and devotion to Mary was widespread in the Church as early as the second century—in other words, from the very beginning. Such devotion was everywhere in the Church, and it left no evidence whatsoever of being controversial, because it wasn't. It was rather accepted as the natural and inevitable corollary of believing that Jesus was God. If Jesus was God, then His Mother was the Theotokos, the Mother of God.

---

18 In Justin's *Dialogue with Trypho*, ch. 100, and Irenaeus' *Against Heresies*, 3.22,4 and *Proof of Apostolic Preaching*, ch. 33.

19 In Tertullian's *On the Flesh of Christ*, ch. 17.

Such a conviction brought with it a devotion of its own. That is why by the mid-third century we find a public prayer offered to Mary, known as the *sub tuum* from its first two words in Latin, which reads, "Beneath your protection we flee for refuge, O Theotokos. Do not disregard our prayers in our adversities, but rescue us from danger, O only pure and blessed one." The plurals used in the prayer (*"we* flee . . . *our* prayers . . . *our* adversities . . . rescue *us"*) witness to its character as a liturgical prayer used in public worship, for private prayers would most likely use the singular (*"I* flee . . . *my* prayers"). This evidence of a flourishing liturgical cult in about AD 250 reveals how widespread devotion to her was, and how deep its roots were in the Church, for devotion must long precede the spread of a public liturgical cult.

We pause to note that this interest in and devotion to Mary was flourishing while the Church was still undergoing fierce persecution from the pagans. This alone makes it utterly unlikely that devotion to Mary represented a transference of devotion from the pagan goddess(es) to Mary. The pagans with their devotion to the pagan goddesses were the enemy, so it was unlikely that the persecuted Christians would borrow from the practices of their persecutors. Rather, just as they saw in the pagan dying and rising gods rivals and mockeries of their faith in the dying and rising Christ, so they would have seen the pagan devotion to their goddesses as rivals and mockeries of the true Mother of God. Appeal to the Christian laxity and supposed syncretism that occurred after Constantine is vain, because Marian devotion was a fixity in the Church long before Constantine was born. Marian devotion was not a pagan import into the Church but grew from the devotional soil of the gospel.

What do Orthodox believe about Mary?

Orthodox believe that she is an *intercessor for all Christians,* regardless of their race, culture, or geographical location. All the disciples of her Son may look to her and find help in her prayers.

There is a difference between an intercessor and a mediator. Christ is the one and only mediator between God and man, as St. Paul teaches in 1 Timothy 2:5. A mediator (Greek *mesites*) is a peacemaker, one who reconciles and brings peace between two estranged or warring parties—in the case of Christ, between God and man, since our sins have alienated us from God. Mary does not function as this kind of mediator, since we have already been reconciled to God through her Son. Rather, she functions as an intercessor.

An intercessor has a wider meaning; it refers to someone who prays for another. When Paul exhorted us to pray for one another and for him (Eph. 6:18–19), he was urging us to be intercessors.

Such intercession, whether coming from Mary, the saints, or ourselves, is rooted in love: we pray and intercede for those we love that God might continue to bless, protect, heal, and rescue them. Since we are members one of another (Eph. 4:25), intercession becomes our duty. In the Church, we are all united one to another in a network of mutual intercession. We pray for each other and rely on those prayers. The question of whether or not God would bless us apart from such intercession does not (or should not) arise: He has commanded us to pray for one another, and we obey. He has chosen to unite us all in one body and to bless us as parts of this prayerful, mutually interceding body. Those intercessors include *all* Christians—even (or especially) the Mother of God.

Orthodox also believe that Mary was *exceptionally holy*. Given that those chosen by God for a particular task are prepared for such work from their mother's womb (such as Jeremiah, Paul, and John the Forerunner; see Jer. 1:5; Gal. 1:15; Luke 1:15), it is inconceivable that Mary should not have been prepared for her task from her mother's womb as well. Jesus was entirely human, with all the inner development expected in men (see Luke 2:52), and that would include being influenced by parental example. Given that Jewish boys spent the first, developmentally crucial years of their lives exclusively with their mothers, we can see how important was Mary's personality and holiness in the rearing of her Son. She had to be an exceptionally holy woman.

It is this holiness that the Orthodox confess when we address her as "all-holy" (Greek *panagia*). This confession of her holiness (expressed in many other terms as well) must be placed within the vocabulary of Scripture. Terms such as "blameless" find their echo in the lives of others as well. Zachariah and Elizabeth, the parents of John the Baptizer, for example, are described by Luke as "righteous before God, walking in all the commandments and ordinances of the Lord blameless" (Luke 1:6). Paul bids the Philippians to be "blameless and harmless, children of God without fault" (Phil. 2:15). Jude also expects Christians, by the power of God, to "stand in the presence of His glory, blameless and with great joy" (Jude 24 NASB). John is bolder still, declaring that Christians purify themselves, just as He is pure, and that "whoever abides in Him does not sin" (1 John 3:3, 6). It is in this conceptual world that we are to locate and understand the blamelessness and holiness of the Lord's Mother.

Closely connected with a belief in Mary's holiness is a belief that after death she received her immense and glorious reward immediately. (This is celebrated in the feast of her Dormition or "falling asleep"—that is, her death.) Orthodox believe that just as she was the first to believe in Christ through the annunciation of the Good News brought to her by the angel Gabriel (Luke 1:26f), so she was the first to receive the reward of glorification in heaven.[20]

Orthodox further confess a belief in Mary's perpetual virginity, praising her as *aeiparthenos*, "ever-virgin." The Scriptures usually used to refute this and assert that Mary had other children are easily explained.

20　See the author's *Re-Discovering Mary* (Alhambra, CA: Sebastian Press, 2021), ch. 9.

In Matthew 1:25, the evangelist declares that Joseph "did not know her till she had brought forth her firstborn Son." From this it is assumed that after Mary gave birth to Jesus, Joseph began to know her (that is, live sexually as man and wife). This is a possible interpretation but not the only valid one. The word rendered "till" is the Greek *eos*. It *can* indicate a change of behavior. If I say, for example, "I will be here until noon," I mean that after the noon hour I will no longer be here. But such a meaning is not required. When the Lord said, "Behold, I am with you always, even until [Greek *eos*] the end of the age" (Matt. 28:20, author's translation), He did not mean that at the end of the age He would no longer be with us. Context is everything.

In Matthew's story of the Lord's Birth, it is clear that the evangelist's sole purpose is to prove that Joseph was not the biological father of Jesus. He could not have been, Matthew says, because he did not touch his betrothed wife until after the child was born. Matthew's interest in the sex life of the Holy Family after that was precisely nil. This text, therefore, has no bearing on the question of Mary's virginity.

It is the same with Luke 2:7, which describes Jesus as Mary's *prototokos*, her "firstborn." This does not imply that she had a second-born or a third-born. The word specifies legal status, not birth order. The prototokos male had a special status under the Law, and thus Mary was required to "redeem" Him (compare Ex. 13:1f). Luke explains that this was part of the reason Mary, Joseph, and Jesus were in Jerusalem, where they were met in the temple by Simeon (Luke 2:22f). Reference to Jesus as the prototokos sets up the birth narrative to explain this meeting in the temple. It has nothing to do with the presence or absence of siblings. The firstborn male would be described as the prototokos even if he were the only child.

The list of our Lord's "brothers" is similarly ambiguous. The word *adelphos* could refer to a sibling of the same mother, but it could equally well indicate any closely related male, such as a stepbrother or cousin. Lot, for example, is referred to in such terms, though he was not Abraham's brother but his nephew (Gen. 12:8; 13:8).

There are some indications in the Gospel accounts that our Lord's brothers mentioned in Mark 6:3 and Matthew 13:55 were in fact His cousins, not children of His Mother. In these two verses they are listed as "James, Joses, Simon, and Judas." When we continue to read those two Gospels, we encounter both sets of names again. The women who stood by the Cross, looking on from a distance, are listed in Matthew 27:55–56 as "Mary Magdalene, Mary the mother of James and Joses, and the mother of Zebedee's sons."

We note that both Matthew and Mark include "Mary the mother of James and Joses" as one of those standing by the Cross, looking on from a distance. It seems clear that the James and Joses mentioned in Matthew 27:56 and Mark 15:40 are the same James and Joses mentioned in Matthew 13:55 and Mark 6:3.

The question here is: Why would Matthew and Mark refer to the Mother of Jesus standing near the Cross as He hung upon it as "Mary the mother of James and Joses" and not as "Mary the mother of Jesus"? The attribution makes no sense. Surely then of all times the evangelists would stress the connection of Mary with her Son. To say that Matthew and Mark referred to Jesus' Mother in that hour as "the mother of James and Joses" is absurd.

The plot thickens as we continue to dig more deeply. In John 19:25, we read that standing by the Cross of Jesus were "His mother, and His mother's sister, Mary the *wife* of Clopas, and Mary Magdalene." We ask: How could Mary the Mother of Jesus have a full sister with the same name of Mary, and who was this Clopas who was important enough to function as the identifier of Jesus' mother's sister?

Eusebius, the fourth-century author of the famous *History*

of the Church, mentions Clopas in this work. Eusebius refers to an earlier history written by Hegesippus, a Jewish Christian writing in the early second century, which relates that Clopas was the brother of Mary's husband, Joseph (*History* 3.11). If this was indeed the case (and Hegesippus was writing within a generation or so of the events themselves), then "Mary the wife of Clopas" was the "sister" of Jesus' Mother in the sense that she was her sister-in-law. Therefore, the three women mentioned in John 19:25 were Jesus' Mother, His aunt, and the devoted Mary Magdalene.

This fits in precisely with the Synoptic accounts. The "Mary the mother of James and Joses" referred to by Matthew and Mark was the "Mary, the wife of Clopas" referred to by John. This being so, James and Joses (along with Judas and Simon) were Jesus' cousins.[21]

If this is denied, then the early tradition that Mary was perpetually virginal needs to be accounted for historically. The Christians who took for granted her virginity and whose assumptions shaped early narratives such as the *Protoevangelium* could read the Gospels as well as anyone. Yet they still insisted, even when James the Lord's brother was prominent as the Bishop of Jerusalem, that Mary was virginal. This insistence only makes sense if they were in possession of a tradition that our Lord's brothers were not His biological siblings. Mary's virginity also accounts for Christ entrusting His Mother not to any one of His brothers (such as James, to whom He would appear after His Resurrection; 1 Cor. 15:7)—a passing over that would have been unthinkable in Jewish culture—but to His close friend, John the Evangelist (John 19:26–27). He did not entrust her to any of her other biological children because she had none—Jesus was an only child. Scripture and history combine to point to the conclusion that Mary was perpetually virginal.

---

21   As suggested by St. Jerome.

Finally, the Orthodox recognize the preeminence of Mary among the saints. Mary is not simply one saint among many. Given her central role in the Incarnation, her importance in raising the Child Jesus, and her chronological primacy in believing the gospel brought by the angel Gabriel, she stands in glory at the head of all the saints as the reward for her faithfulness.

She is, in fact, the spiritual mother of all her Son's disciples, mother of the Church. If Deborah arose as a mother in Israel, leading the way to victory and salvation (Judg. 4:4–5), Mary functions as a mother in messianic Israel, the Church. That is the mystical meaning of our Lord giving her as a mother to St. John (John 19:27). In doing so, Christ was not simply asking John to take care of His Mother after He was gone. Saint John functions in his own Gospel as the beloved disciple, the ideal Christian, an image of the Church. In giving His Mother to John, Christ was giving her to all His disciples. Every Christian therefore can look to Mary as a mother, a protector, an intercessor, a source of comfort and love.

CHAPTER FOUR

More Joy in Heaven

The Saints

If Evangelicals see no need for the intercession of Mary and regard such Marian devotion as sinful, the same goes for the saints. Some Evangelicals may speak about St. Paul rather than simply Paul, but the reluctance to ascribe more holiness to one Christian than another remains, and the notion that some Christians might be closer to God in the Kingdom than others and therefore might have greater powers of intercession remains foreign to them. In their view, Christians on earth do not need and cannot benefit from the intercession of those gone before any more than they could do so from the intercession of the Mother of Jesus—and for the same reason: salvation consists entirely of being forgiven at the moment of conversion, and the prayers of the saints form no part of this transaction.

Indeed, talk about the saints does not sit comfortably in evangelical theology. Evangelicals believe (correctly) that all true Christians are saints (compare 1 Cor. 1:2; Eph. 1:1), and so the creation of a separate category of "capital S saints" is regarded as unbiblical and problematic. This is especially so when those saints are the recipients of special devotion from the faithful. Such devotion, like devotion to Mary, is often regarded as the importation of paganism into the Church—gods and goddesses once worshipped by pagans as deities are now worshipped by Christians as saints. Prayer to them and devotion to their images are therefore strictly prohibited.[22] Their pictures are never found adorning the walls of evangelical churches.

In fact, the practice of venerating the saints and asking for their intercession began almost immediately in the early Church in that it was always a part of the Church's attitude toward its martyrs. After Polycarp, the aged bishop of Smyrna, was martyred in 155, eyewitnesses wrote an account of the event. Part of it reads, "Later on we took up his bones, which are more valuable than precious stones and finer than refined gold, and deposited them in a suitable place. There, when we gather together as we are able, with joy and gladness, the Lord will permit us to celebrate the birthday of his martyrdom in commemoration of those who have already fought in the contest and also for the training and preparation of those who will do so in the future" (*Martyrdom of Polycarp*, chapter 19).

We see from this account that the relics or remains of the martyred saint were treasured and kept for veneration. We also note an immediate cult of the martyr, in which the church gathered around his place of burial to celebrate the Eucharist and read the story of his martyrdom, both to honor the martyr and "in training and preparation" of those who will be martyred in the immediate future. It was understood that prayers addressed to the martyr would be answered and that his relics were a source of blessing and power.

Note, too, the date: AD 155. This cult of honoring the martyrs thus began as soon as the Church began producing such martyrs—in other words, long before anyone might have thought of importing the cult of pagan gods into the Church. The veneration

---

22 Protestant churches that retain "saints' days" (such as the Anglican Church) only refer to the saints as examples and never offer prayer to them.

of saints (beginning with the martyrs) sprang naturally from the Church's theological conviction that those in heaven were not separated from those still on earth and would pray for them.

Granted that the practice of asking the martyrs and saints for their prayers arose early in the Church, we may still ask how and why it arose. We therefore need to read closely the texts produced by the Jews of the centuries immediately before Christ in order to discern from them the underlying presuppositions that the Christians inherited from Judaism. And when we do this, we see that the Jews of the time assumed that those in heaven had knowledge of what was happening on earth and were praying for them.

Thus, for example, we read in 2 Maccabees 15:12[23] that the martyred high priest Onias "was praying with outstretched hands for the whole body of the Jews" (RSV). Moreover, he was joined in his intercession by a man "distinguished by his gray hair and dignity, and of marvelous majesty and authority." Onias revealed in the vision that "This is a man who loves the brethren and prays much for the people and the holy city, Jeremiah, the prophet of God" (vv. 13–14).

We see the same conviction that those in heaven prayed for those on earth in the Book of Enoch, a composite work dating from the first century.[24] Thus in Enoch 9:3 we read, "To you, the holy ones of heaven, the souls of men make their suit, saying, 'Bring our cause before the Most High.'" Later on, in Enoch 39:5, we find the same idea that those in heaven were praying for those on earth: "My eyes saw the dwellings [of the holy] with His holy angels and they petitioned and interceded and prayed for the children of men." In Enoch 99:3, the righteous on earth are told to

---

23 The three Books of the Maccabees, which record events that occurred in the second century BC, are included in Orthodox Bibles. Protestants consider them "apocrypha."

24 The Book of Enoch is not included in the Orthodox canon but is considered worthy to be read by individuals.

"raise your prayers as a memorial, and place them as a testimony before the angels, that they may place the sin of the sinner for a memorial before the Most High." In Enoch 104:1 we read that "in heaven the angels remember you for good before the glory of the Great One." These texts reveal that at least some Jews in the first century believed that the angels in heaven were praying for those on earth and presenting their prayers to God. Those in heaven— Onias, Jeremiah, and the angels—were intimately involved in what was happening on earth.

This assumption clearly lies behind our Lord's words that there is more joy in heaven over the repentance of a single sinner on earth than over many who do not need to repent (Luke 15:7), for how could those in heaven know of the sinner's repentance unless earth somehow lay open to their gaze? The same assumption also undergirds the image found in Hebrews 12:1, which uses an athletic race to portray the Christian struggle. We on earth are running the race of faith, cheered on by a "great cloud of witnesses" observing us from the heavenly stands.

And then there is the Book of Revelation. This text must be used carefully, with a full recognition of its special genre. It does not offer a literal behind-the-scenes peek at what is going on in heaven, as if a journalist were allowed to wander around backstage behind the curtain. But it does reveal the assumptions held by the Church at the time regarding the state of those in heaven. From this we learn that the angels brought the prayers of those on earth to God (Rev. 8:3–4)—exactly as the Book of Enoch said. Regarding the departed Christians, we learn that they are with Christ and are being comforted by Him for their struggles on earth (7:13f). We also learn that they seem to know what is happening on earth: in 6:9–11 they clamour impatiently for judgment to be poured out on their oppressors, and in 16:4–7 they exult after the judgment has been poured out. It is clear from this that they know what is happening on earth while they are in heaven.

We may conclude from this close reading of the texts of the time that it was part of the Church's faith in the first century that those in heaven—departed saints as well as angels—interceded for those on earth.

This intimate unity of the saints in heaven with the saints still on earth found increased strength through the Resurrection of Christ, for by His Resurrection He abolished death (2 Tim. 1:10). This not only means that death cannot separate us from Christ; it also means that death can no longer separate Christians from one another. If the living and departed are both united to Christ, they are by virtue of this union also united to one another. Even while on earth all Christians are united in a bond of mutual prayer and intercession (Eph. 6:18)—how much more will our departed brethren pray for us when they are closer to Christ in heaven? Salvation consists of sharing the glory of Christ and becoming by grace what He is by nature (Rom. 8:29). This means that we share not only His sonship but also His heavenly glory, being continually transformed from one degree of glory to another (2 Cor. 3:18). If we share His glory in this life, how much more in the next, when righteous men are made perfect (Heb. 12:23)? Salvation involves theosis, as we share the very glory of Christ and are "*co*-glorified with Him" (Rom. 8:17, author's translation).[25]

In summary, the New Testament lays the foundation for the invocation of saints, witnessing to the union of heaven with earth and teaching that Christians will share the heavenly glory of Christ in the next life. With this theology, it was natural and inevitable that Christians would ask for the prayers of the saints and martyrs. This theology and practice continues today in the Orthodox Church. Orthodox venerate the saints, asking for their prayers, honoring their icons, and treasuring their relics. As they

---

25 The Greek reads not *doxazo*, but *sundoxazo*. The word indicates not a glorification *like* that of Christ but a sharing in Christ's very glorification.

are our brothers and sisters in the Faith who stand in the presence of Christ and share His glory, Orthodox Christians rely upon the saints' prayers, knowing these prayers to be the conduits of Christ's saving grace.

CHAPTER FIVE

"Asleep in Jesus, blessed sleep"

Praying for the Dead

Evangelicals do not pray for those who have died. When an Evangelical dies, his evangelical friends and family, assuming that the departed is with the Lord, give thanks for this but do not pray for the departed. That is because the only thing that matters for them is whether or not the departed was born again and forgiven his or her sins before he or she died. If this has taken place, there is nothing more that needs to be done or can be done. Salvation consists of getting to heaven after death, and since the departed is now in heaven, nothing else needs to be accomplished. The purpose of the funeral is to comfort the survivors on the loss of their friend or family member and assure everyone that the departed is now at rest with the Lord in heaven.

Evangelicals therefore look on the practice of praying for the Christian dead as evidence that those surviving are not sure the departed was saved and is now in heaven. Worse yet, the prayers could be read as evidence that the Church on earth can somehow pray the departed *into* heaven, changing his fate after he has died from damnation to salvation; this possibility is of course hotly denied. The dead are either saved or damned, in heaven or in hell, and there is nothing the Church on earth can do about it.

But the Church has always prayed for its Christian dead. Such prayers do not loom large on the pages of the New Testament, but that is to be expected of a document written in the first years of the Church's life, when only a few Christians had died. Even so, we are told that our departed loved ones are with the Lord (1 Thess. 4:13f), and we have a brief prayer of St. Paul for one who had died—Onesiphorus, to whom Paul refers in the past tense and for whose surviving household he prays. Paul prays that he may "find mercy from the Lord in that Day" of judgment (2 Tim. 1:16–18).

Such prayer for the dead is not surprising, for the Judaism out of which Christianity arose knew of prayer for the dead. In 2 Maccabees 12:41f, we read of pious Jews offering prayer for the forgiveness of fellow Jews who have died, and there is no reason Christians would have rejected such a practice. Indeed, the history of the Church proves that they did not, for intercession for the dead has always formed a part of the Church's liturgical life.

The Church has always believed that the souls of Christians who have lived in piety and true discipleship, through the mercy of Christ and the prayers of His Church, will come to dwell "in a place of brightness, a place of refreshment, a place of repose, where all sickness, sorrow, and sighing have fled away" (from the Orthodox funeral service). We do know that for the faithful to depart this life is to be at home with Christ (2 Cor. 5:8; Phil. 1:23). What we do *not* know are the mechanics, the details of the journey, the process of self-knowledge and purification that occurs on the other side, and the map of celestial geography.

There is nothing inherently wrong with the concept that a soul must be purified after death, if this purification is divorced from the forensic demands of justice and tied more closely to therapeutic healing. Our passions impede us from fully experiencing the presence and power of God, which alone bring joy. If we are to experience joy to the full—what St. Paul refers to as "a weight of glory" (2 Cor. 4:17)—it makes sense that an inner transformation will be necessary, removing all the inner barriers to

God's presence that we have foolishly erected. Seen in this light, unacknowledged impatience, anger, lust, resentment, or other sins lurking within us need to be acknowledged and removed before we can experience joy to the full. These sins are not so much debts we must pay off by suffering before God can bless us and admit us to heaven, as dark spots on the windows of our soul that must be removed before the divine light can fully flood into us. No doubt seeing our sins in all their ugliness and consenting to the removal of things that have become so much a part of us may be painful. No one likes to hear unpleasant things about himself, even in this life. The process of purification and of spiritual surgery therefore may be accompanied by some pain. But the pain is not the point. It is incidental to the real goal, which is ridding ourselves of the cancer growing within us so that we can experience God in freedom and joy.

It is here that our prayers on earth for the departed can be of some help. The ability to dwell fully in a place of brightness, a place of refreshment, a place of repose depends on the state of the heart. It is a matter of the departed attaining spiritual health, not of their finding their way to a particular piece of celestial real estate. In the words of C. S. Lewis in *The Last Battle*, we go further up and further in, journeying eternally onward (if St. Gregory of Nyssa is to be believed) in an endless ascent of joy.

Our prayers for the departed cannot take the place of their repentance in this life if they entered the next life entirely unrepentant. But they can perhaps help those who do enter the next life repentant and ready to undergo further repentance if shown the truth about themselves. To be completely and peacefully at home in a place of brightness, refreshment, and repose, the soul must have some inner brightness, freshness, and rest within itself. It is for this that the Church offers confident prayer for its Christian departed, certain that the loving Lord will bring peace and joy to those who have entered His presence.

CHAPTER SIX

"Call no man 'Father'"

The Role of the Parish Clergy

In most evangelical churches, the main pastor functions primarily as a preacher. That is, his or her role consists mainly of preaching the sermon on Sundays. The day-to-day tasks of visitation and pastoral care devolve not on him but on others. The work of caring for the youth or producing the music on Sundays is given over to other pastors, often called the youth pastor or the music pastor. Despite the common title of *pastor*, these are clearly subordinate ministries and roles to that of the main or senior pastor.

The senior pastor is accountable ultimately to the congregation and not to any external church authority, such as a bishop or superintendent—that is, he is accountable to a church board. It is this board that first hired him and can fire him, subject to certain rules and conditions. It is estimated that the average length of time a pastor stays in a congregation is about five years, though of course there are exceptions. The final authority in evangelical churches lies with the church board, which is usually elected by the congregation at an annual general meeting. Decisions about the spending of money, the type of music used in church, and congregational discipline are ultimately in their hands.

That said, obviously, given the immense variety found among evangelical congregations and the difference in pastoral personalities, some pastors will have more independence and authority than others. Indeed, in most churches, the vision and even the doctrine of the senior pastor becomes the standard for that church, and he is not bound by any external standard of doctrine but his own. The mode of governance used in evangelical churches has changed dramatically over the past decades and is still in flux. The variety of the internal political dynamics found within evangelical churches can scarcely be overstated.

In the Orthodox Church, the local pastor (or presbyter, from the Greek *presbyteros*, or "elder") is often called a priest, since he normally presides over the Eucharist, which is regarded as sacrificial. The local priest is ultimately responsible not to the local board or parish council but to his bishop. Of course the priest will work with his parish council and is in some measure responsible to them and to the parish for his actions. But discipline and assignment (i.e., hiring and firing) remain solely in the hands of the bishop, to whom both priest and parish are responsible. Moreover, the priest cannot determine the standard of orthodoxy or set doctrine according to his own views. Instead he is bound to hold and preach only the Orthodox Faith, the Faith held by all the Orthodox and preserved by his own bishop. Each priest, therefore, teaches the same doctrine and holds to the same Faith.[26]

The priest is the locus of authority in the parish, though finances remain the responsibility of the parish council (and, for large expenditures, the congregation as a whole). Decisions about services, music, discipline of members, and the general direction of the congregation lie with the priest. Nothing in the parish can be accomplished apart from his blessing, though naturally a wise priest will work with his parish council.

In other words, the priest is a father to his parish, functioning

---

26 That is why priests' individuality is not stressed and why they all dress the same, wearing a black cassock. What matters is not their differing individuality but their common Faith.

in the same way that a father functions in his family (or, at least, as he did in more classical times). He is honored by the people, so that he is the one who opens and closes meetings with prayer, who says grace at parish mealtimes. He is also greeted with a ritual of blessing: when greeting a priest (or a bishop), one will hold out one's upturned palms and say "Father, bless!" The priest will sign the person with the cross and drop his hand into the upturned palms for the person to kiss the hand that blessed her.

Given this paternal role of the parish clergy, it is not surprising the priest is addressed with the honorific title "Father."[27] It is just here that many Evangelicals object. Addressing a priest as "Father," they argue, contradicts a command of the Lord Jesus, who ordered that Christians "call no man father." However, this interpretation of Matthew 23:9 is not correct; our Lord does not forbid the use of the honorific.

Admittedly, the Good News Bible, the Living Bible, and the New International Version all render the verse "you must not call anyone here on earth 'Father.'" More accurate versions such as the King James and NKJV, the RSV, and the New American Standard do not render it this way, since the Greek reads *patera me kalesete **umon** epi tes ges*. Note the boldface **umon**, so that the verse is rendered more accurately as "call no man **your** father on the earth" (thus, e.g., KJV).

What is the difference between "call no man father" and "call no man your father"? It is the difference between a title or form of address and a relationship. It is the latter Christ is describing and proscribing, not the former. The Bible never says "call no man father." Indeed, such a command would be bizarre in a Middle Eastern environment, where the term "father" was the usual honorific for a male person of mature age. That is why the term is on the lips even of the rich man in Christ's parable: he calls the

---

27 The honorific is not confined to priests; lay monks, for example, are also addressed as "Father" and nuns as "Mother."

venerable patriarch "Father Abraham" when he calls out to him for help (Luke 16:24, 30).

Christ's word about never calling anyone on the earth one's father finds its true meaning in the context of His denunciation of the Pharisees and the rabbinic piety of the time. This is why the command shows up in Matthew's very Jewish Gospel and not (for example) in the Gospel of Luke, which was addressed to a Gentile audience.

One of the practices Christ warned His disciples to avoid was the insistence on public honor and loyalty. The Pharisees loved respectful greetings in public and being hailed with the title "rabbi" (literally, "my master/my great one". The term "rabbi" at that time was another honorific; it did not denote a clerical office as it does today.) The rabbis would accumulate disciples, men whose task it was to memorize the views and words of their rabbi and make them their own. Indeed, those teachers claimed a greater respect from their disciples than was due to one's parents. They reasoned that parents gave only earthly life, while the rabbinic teacher gave spiritual and eternal life. The rabbis functioned therefore as gurus for those who followed them as their personal disciples.

Our Lord insisted that such total allegiance and blind loyalty had no place among His followers in His Church. The leaders in His movement were never to function as that kind of father, commanding personal allegiance and accumulating personal disciples. Such complete allegiance could only be given to God, their common Father in heaven. On earth the only Leader to whom such devotion should be given was Christ, the Messiah of all. His disciples were all brothers, and even the leaders among them looked to the same Leader and Lord, the Christ of God (Matt. 23:8–10).

In all this, what mattered was where the heart was and to whom one gave ultimate loyalty. The rabbis of the Pharisees claimed personal loyalty from their disciples as their due in a kind of personality cult. Such a cult and such devotion were to find no place among Jesus' followers. The issue was not so much whether one calls one's leader "Father Tom" or "Pastor Tom." The issue was the relationship between the leader and the led. One can be led by Father Tom and address him as Father Tom. But Father Tom can never command ultimate personal loyalty—nor, as a true disciple of Christ, would he wish to. Christ is our earthly Leader, and He has taught us that God in heaven is our Father. We therefore call no man on earth our true and life-giving father apart from Him.

This paternal role of the priest and his authority within the congregation has its roots in the New Testament. There the local leader is called an "elder" (Greek *presbyteros*), in which role he functioned with other elders within the same city. He is also called an *episkopos* (Greek for "bishop" or "overseer").[28] The main function of the presbyter was to rule—that is, he exercised real authority within the congregation, both to lead the worship, to teach, and to administer discipline (see 1 Tim. 3:1–5; 5:17).

The presbyter/teacher was also called a *poimen*, a shepherd (Eph. 4:11). The term "shepherd" is a term of authority in the ancient world, used to describe kings and rulers, who ruled their peoples as a shepherd ruled his flock. Thus God is the true shepherd of Israel (Ezek. 34:11f). The use of the term to describe the presbyters and teachers in the congregation similarly speaks to their authority as well as to their care for their flock.

It is because of this real and paternal authority over the people that Christians are exhorted to obey their leaders and submit to

---

28 It is apparent from Acts 20:17, 28 and Titus 1:5, 7 that the two titles were used interchangeably. Later in the first century the title of "bishop" would be reserved for the main elder/bishop in a community, who always had the central role of coordinating the others. In Jerusalem that leader was James.

them, for they keep watch over their souls (Heb. 13:17). It was natural for such men to be addressed as "Father" and to be regarded as a conduit of divine blessing.

CHAPTER SEVEN

"Give me that old-time religion"

Continuity and Worship

Evangelical worship is quite varied, but certain common elements still prevail: it is usually informal and relaxed; it is usually non-eucharistic (though this increasingly varies as the Lord's Supper is now served more often); and it is largely non-liturgical—that is, the words used are not prescribed and set down in a book. These characteristics are the fruit of a common historical root—namely, a rejection of the Church's practice in centuries past. The worship of that pre-Reformation Church was formal, eucharistic, and liturgical, and so Evangelicals have classically reacted against this by insisting on worship that is *in*formal, *non*-eucharistic and *non*-liturgical.

It was axiomatic among the churches of the Reformation that the Catholic Church had become so debased and its worship so corrupted that it was no longer the Church. Instead, the Catholic Church had become Babylon the Great, mother of harlots and of the abominations of the earth (see Rev. 17:5). It was important for Protestants in reestablishing the original and true worship of the early Church to reject anything that savored of the Catholic corruptions.[29]

---

29 Thus some Puritans in England even wanted to reject the use of the ring in the marriage ceremony.

Inheriting this tradition, most evangelical church services are informal, with casual conversation, comment, and banter happening between the officiants and the congregation. That is, words are spoken throughout the service that are not prescribed in a book or text. Though there is structure to the service, words and prayers are usually spontaneous, being made up in the moment.

Also, the usual Sunday morning service is not the Lord's Supper—it is not a designated "Communion Sunday." Instead it consists of music (either hymns or choruses, often led by a praise band located at the front of the church on a stage), a reading from Scripture, a prayer offered, and a long address or sermon, which forms the centerpiece of the service.

Often sophisticated technology is employed, not excluding the use of slides for the sermons, and sometimes in larger churches even a smoke machine to augment the musical display by the praise band.

Services exhibit great variety, according to the preferences of pastor and congregation, the size of the church, and the money available for technology. Smaller congregations tend to be more conservative liturgically, retaining the use of hymnbooks and an organ or piano. They are more likely to sing "Blessed assurance, Jesus is mine" than the latest praise chorus and to prefer time-honored structure to inventive creativity.

Some churches make use of more traditional elements, such as using candles as aids for focus in prayer or in Advent wreaths. But there are limits to such borrowings: usages savoring of Catholic liturgy, such as statues of saints and saying the rosary, would be unwelcome. Within these anti-Catholic limits, almost any variety is allowed, although custom results in a service consisting of songs, prayer, the taking of an offering, and a sermon.

By contrast, the Orthodox Church retains its pre-Reformation characteristics, so that its liturgy is formal,[30] liturgical, and eucha-

---

30 This formality should not be overstressed, for Orthodox worship is

ristic. This is because, unlike the Protestant inheritance under-lying Evangelicalism, Orthodoxy never repudiated its theological or liturgical past. Instead, it accepted the past and built on it.

Orthodox worship therefore represents an enlargement and refinement of the original liturgy of the early and patristic Church rather than its rejection. Reformation Protestantism rejected its liturgical past, seeking to recover an earlier and purer worship that existed before it was corrupted. Orthodoxy believes that the inheritance of the early Church never suffered corruption, and so it sought to preserve this inheritance and enhance it.

Here it is instructive to peer back into that early Church inheritance to see what worship was like then. In those early days, there was of course no set text used by all the churches, and some variety existed in the liturgical tradition. But the structure of worship and its meaning were the same everywhere.

An example of that structure can be recovered from the description of Justin Martyr, who died in about 165 in Rome. In his first *Apology* or defense of the Christian Faith, he described the worship of the Church in order to assure his pagan readers that, contrary to rumor, Christians did not practice cannibalism or incestuous orgies at their services.[31] In chapters 65–67 of his *Apology*, he wrote as follows:

> But we, after we have thus washed him [in baptism], we
> bring him to the place where those who are called "brothers"

---

relaxed as well as formal. Compare the observations of C. S. Lewis on the Russian Orthodox worship he experienced at Oxford: "Some stood, some knelt, some sat, some walked. . . . And the beauty of it was that nobody took the slightest notice of what anyone else was doing" (from his *Letters to Malcolm* [New York: Mariner Books, 2012], 10).

31 Such rumors were based on reports of Christians "eating the body and drinking the blood" and on their exchange of "the kiss" of peace among "the brothers and the sisters."

are assembled, in order that we may offer hearty prayers in common for ourselves and for the illuminated [baptized] person, and for all others in every place. . . . Having ended the prayers, we salute one another with a kiss. There is then brought to the president of the brothers bread and a cup of wine mixed with water; and he taking them, gives praise and glory to the Father of the universe, through the name of the Son and of the Holy Spirit, and offers thanks at considerable length for our being counted worthy to receive these things at His hands. And when he has concluded the prayers and thanksgivings, all the people present express their assent by "Amen." . . . And when the president has given thanks, and all the people have expressed their assent, those who are called by us "deacons" give to each of those present to partake of the bread and wine mixed with water over which the thanksgiving was pronounced, and to those who are absent they carry away a portion.

And this food is called among us the Eucharist, of which no one is allowed to partake but the man who believes that the things which we teach are true, and who has been washed with the washing that is for the remission of sins, and unto rebirth, and who is so living as Christ has enjoined. For not as common bread and common drink do we receive these; but in like manner as Jesus Christ our Savior, having been made flesh by the Word of God, had both flesh and blood for our salvation, so likewise have we been taught that the food which is blessed by the prayer of His word, and from which our blood and flesh by transmutation are nourished, is the flesh and blood of that Jesus who was made flesh. For the apostles, in the memoirs composed by them, which are called "Gospels," have thus delivered unto us what was enjoined upon them; that Jesus took bread, and when He had given thanks, said, "Do this is remembrance of Me. This is My body." And that, after the same manner, having taken the cup and given thanks, He said, "This is My blood," and gave it to them alone.

And we afterwards continually remind each other of these things. . . . And on the day called Sunday, all who live in cities or in the country gather together to one place, and the memoirs of the apostles or the writings of the prophets are read, as long as time permits; then, when the reader has ceased, the president verbally instructs, and exhorts to the imitation of these good things. Then we all rise together and pray, and, as we before said, when our prayer is ended, bread and wine and water are brought, and the president in like manner offers prayers and thanksgivings, according to his ability, and the people assent, saying "Amen"; and there is a distribution to each, and a participation of that over which thanks have been given, and to those who are absent a portion is sent by the deacons.[32]

Despite the literary toing and froing of the descriptions, it is possible to reconstruct the structure of the service. In list form it would be:

> » Assembly of the baptized
> » Readings from the Bible
> » Verbal instruction/sermon by the one presiding[33]
> » Prayers "for ourselves and for all others in every place"
> » Kiss of peace
> » Bringing in of bread and wine mixed with water
> » Prayer over the bread and cup by the one presiding

---

32 Ante-Nicene Fathers, ed. Roberts and Donaldson, vol. 1 (Grand Rapids, MI: Wm. B. Eerdmans Publishing, 1977), 185–186.

33 That is, by the bishop; Justin hides the title behind the description "the one presiding" to protect the bishop from persecution.

> » Distribution of the bread and cup to all, received as Christ's Body and Blood, including
> » Distribution to those absent by the deacons

It is significant that this order and structure is later found in every single eucharistic service the world over. There are no exceptions. This invariability and universality witness to the apostolic source of this structure—it was the apostles themselves who regulated what was to be done at the assembly of the Christians early on Sunday morning.[34] This being so, the Church recognized that it had no authority to alter something so fundamental that was set down by the apostolic founders. Certain things could be added—such as psalms sung after assembling, which were once sung on the way to church,[35] or the Creed,[36] or certain entrances into the altar area[37]—but nothing set down by the apostles could be omitted or taken away.

This apostolic structure and content still form the liturgical backbone of the Eucharist in the Orthodox Church to this day. Other services have been added (such as Vespers in the evening and Matins in the morning), but the main gathering of the Christians on Sunday morning is still that of the Eucharist.

---

34 This is all the more certain when we reflect that originally the bread and cup were consecrated and shared as part of an evening meal (see 1 Cor. 11). If there were no apostolic involvement, one would have expected great variety in the structure and content of the morning Eucharist following its first-century separation from the evening agape meal. The fact that there *was* no such variety of content—or controversy about it—witnesses to the fact that the content and structure originated with the apostles.

35 The three so-called antiphons sung at the beginning of the Byzantine Liturgy.

36 Originally recited only at baptisms.

37 After the church had built larger buildings which could accommodate such entrances.

The formality that attends this service is the result of the Christians knowing what they are doing—namely, eating and drinking the Body and Blood of the Incarnate God. Such an awe-inspiring event precludes lighthearted levity and inculcates a degree of joyful solemnity. At the Eucharist the Christians rejoice, but they rejoice with trembling (see Ps. 2:11). This solemnity also dictates what accompaniments are appropriate to such an event—the use of clowns, Halloween costumes, or smoke machines such as are used in rock concerts are all excluded.[38] All liturgical additions must be consistent with the spirit of the apostolic liturgical core, and no addition must be allowed to usurp the centrality of the eucharistic prayer and the reception of Holy Communion as the climax of the rite.

We also mention three other elements of the apostolic pattern of worship that are rooted in Orthodoxy's desire to preserve that pattern.

The first is that of orientation. That is, from the days of the apostles, Christians have always faced east when they pray (a clear alternative to facing Jerusalem for prayer, and a change made by the apostles in the first century following the separation of the Church from the synagogue). Saint Basil mentions this custom as an ordinance of the apostles in his book *On the Holy Spirit*, chapter 27.[39]

Second is that the usual posture for prayer is standing, not kneeling. This is attested in our Lord's words in Mark 11:25, which reads, "whenever you stand praying . . . forgive." Note: It is *taken for granted* by Christ that prayer will be offered standing (see also Luke 18:11)—Christ here adds that when one stands praying, one must also forgive. Kneeling or prostrating in prayer

---

38 These examples are not inventions; the author has seen services in which all have been used.

39 St. Basil the Great, *On the Holy Spirit* (Crestwood, NY: SVS Press, 1980), 100.

was a sign of intense emotion (as experienced by Paul in Acts 20:36 and by Christ in Mark 14:35). Such kneeling or prostration was therefore seen as penitential, which is why it was forbidden during the joyful season of Pascha by the canons of the Council of Nicea. That is also why traditional Orthodox churches do not have pews.

Finally, the original eucharistic gatherings in the homes of the Christians did not include musical instrumentation, and so when the gathering was transferred to buildings specially built for Christian worship (that is, to churches), musical instruments continued not to be used. This large topic is dealt with at greater length in Appendix B.

CHAPTER EIGHT

"Come to the Table"

The Meaning of the Eucharist

Evangelicals are emphatic that the service of the Lord's Supper or Communion as they perform it is radically different in meaning and significance from the service as found in the pre-Reformation Catholic Church. Indeed, one might almost say the Catholic assertions about the Mass set the stage for the Reformation denials. The Catholic Church declared that the service of the Lord's Supper or the Mass was sacrificial in that the true Sacrifice of Christ was manifest on the altar and that the bread and wine received were the real and saving Body and Blood of Christ.

These two assertions were heatedly denied at the Reformation[40] and continue to be heatedly denied by all Evangelicals. The latter believe that the service of the Lord's Supper was instituted to remind the faithful that Christ had died for them, and the consumption of bread and wine (often substituted with crackers and grape juice) are merely visual reminders of this. The bread and wine are in no real sense Christ's Body and Blood, and they undergo no saving change at all in the service.

This is often stressed at the Communion service, sometimes expressed by referring to the bread and wine as "emblems" or

---

40 Luther confessed the eucharistic bread and wine to be Christ's Body and Blood but vociferously denied they were sacrificial.

"symbols" to make clear that they do not become Christ's Body and Blood. Evangelicals regard the notion that the Mass is a sacrifice as blasphemous and a denial of the once-for-all saving nature of Christ's Sacrifice on the Cross.

Evangelicals insist that the Lord's Supper, often conducted with great devotion and dignity, contributes nothing to one's salvation and offers no remission of sins, either to the living or the dead. Its value consists of being a devotional reminder of the historical death of Jesus on the Cross and of the price He paid there for our salvation. This accounts for its infrequent occurrence in many churches, with some congregations having a Communion service only four times a year.[41] It also accounts for the casual approach of some congregations to its celebration and reception.

As Orthodoxy retained the original apostolic *structure* of the Eucharist, so it retained its *meaning*. The Orthodox Church retains the understanding of the Eucharist held by the early and patristic Church—namely, that it is a true sacrifice in which the faithful receive Christ's Body and Blood under the forms of bread and wine, for the remission of their sins and for eternal life.

The Eucharist is sacrificial not because in it Christ is sacrificed or immolated again but because in it, by the power of the Holy Spirit and in obedience to Christ's command, the Church makes a memorial of Him and His sacrifice.

This biblical concept of memorial, remembrance, and memory has been misunderstood in Protestantism. For Protestants, the command "This do in remembrance of Me" (Luke 22:19 KJV) is interpreted through a modern and unbiblical understanding of what a memorial is. In this modern misunderstanding, remembrance and memory are seen as functions of the mind: remembering refers to a mental activity inside one's brain, like daydreaming—except that daydreaming involves the present or the

---

41 As said above, there is great variety among evangelical churches regarding the frequency of holding a Communion service.

future, whereas remembering involves the past. But both remembering and daydreaming are strictly mental activities.

It is otherwise in the Bible. Several examples may be helpful to illustrate the biblical notion of remembering.

In Numbers 10, God commanded Moses to make two silver trumpets. These were to be blown when the camp was to gather and to set out. They were also to be blown "when you go to war in your land against the enemy who oppresses you, then you shall sound an alarm with the trumpets, and you will be remembered before the Lord your God, and you will be saved from your enemies" (Num. 10:9). The trumpets were also to be blown over their sacrifices, "and they shall be as a memorial of you before your God" (v. 10). The Hebrew for "remember" and "memorial" are *zakar* and its cognate *zikaron*.

Here the concept of "remembering" and "memorial" is that of doing something so that *God may remember you*—and when God remembers, He always takes action. When He remembered Israel because they made a memorial by blowing the trumpets in a time of war, He took action by saving them from their enemies.

We see this concept of remembrance working negatively in 1 Kings 17:18. Elijah had come to stay with a woman who had given him shelter. When her young son suddenly died, she rounded on him and demanded, "Have you come to me to bring my sin to remembrance [Heb. *zakar*], and to kill my son?" When God remembers iniquity, He does not simply recall it in His head but takes action and brings judgment. Remembrance always involves action.[42] (In this case, her son's death was *not* the result of God remembering her iniquity, nor was it permanent.)

We see this same concept of remembrance and memorial in the New Testament. In Acts 10:4, Cornelius is told by an angel that his prayers and alms have ascended "for a memorial [Greek

---

42 We see the same understanding of remembrance functioning in Isaiah 62:6–7 (RSV).

eis mneosunon] before God"—that is, they functioned as would a memorial offering. The meaning is the same as that of the Greek *anamnesis*, the word used in the Septuagint of Leviticus 24:7, where it describes a memorial portion of the showbread. Here in Acts 10:4, the angel tells Cornelius that his acts of piety have functioned in the same way as a memorial offering, so that God has now remembered him and is sending Peter to him with a divine message. Once again, a memorial (Heb. *zakar, zikaron*; Greek *mneosunon, anamnesis*) refers to *something done so that God may remember* and take action.

This is what our Lord established at the Last Supper: eating bread and drinking wine at the gathering of His people served as an anamnesis of Him and His sacrifice. In Luke 22:19, He says that His disciples should do this *eis ten emen anamnesin*—"for My memorial." It is this action that will cause God to remember Him and His sacrifice and bring it into their midst—not by way of repetition of the sacrifice but through anamnesis. That is why the bread and wine His people consume are also His Body and Blood.

We see this dual notion of sacrifice and the Real Presence of His Body and Blood in the writings of Paul.

In 1 Corinthians 10, St. Paul warns his readers not to eat food that has been offered to idols, since eating such food would bring them into communion with the deities to whom the food had been offered. This is the same principle, he explains, that was operative in the Old Testament: to eat food offered to the Lord made the Israelites "partakers of the altar," so that they thereby experienced communion with the Lord to whom the sacrifices were made (v. 18). Paul clarified that he did not mean that the gods of the pagans to whom sacrifices were offered were true gods, but rather that they were demons, and that Christians could not share the cup of the Lord at the Eucharist while also sharing the cup of demons by eating sacrifices offered to idols.

He then summed up by saying, "You cannot partake of the table of the Lord [at the Eucharist] and of the table of demons" (v. 21 ESV). The word rendered "table" is the Greek *trapeza*. The "trapeza of the demons" was the sacrificial altar on which the sacrifice to the idols was offered—and therefore the "trapeza of the Lord" must be sacrificial as well. A table, in this context, is also an altar, something on which a sacrifice is offered. Paul uses this parallel, comparing the Eucharist to both the altar of the idols and the Old Testament altar of God, because the eucharistic table is an altar as well. The Eucharist is clearly sacrificial.

In 1 Corinthians 10, Paul also reminds his readers of the holiness of what they receive every Sunday at the Eucharist, intending thereby to curb their irreverent behavior at the Supper. He asks, "Is not the cup of blessing which we bless a sharing in the blood of Christ? Is not the bread which we break a sharing in the body of Christ?" (v. 16 LSB). The word here rendered "sharing" is the Greek *koinonia*. It refers to someone participating in something.[43] For example, if I passed my cup of coffee around to everyone and all drank from it, this would be their *koinonia* in the coffee.

Note that the bread and wine here are called Christ's Body and Blood. That this was not simply a metaphor is proven by the warning St. Paul gives in 1 Corinthians 11:27. There he warns them that to eat and drink of the bread and cup unworthily is to be "guilty of the body and blood of the Lord"—something sufficiently terrible that those guilty of this sin have become sick, and some have even died (vv. 27–30). No one suffers such a penalty from insufficient appreciation of a metaphor. The Lord's Body and Blood are truly present in the bread and the cup, and it is the sin against them that brings such a terrible penalty.

The careful reader can find this same understanding of the saving nature of the Eucharist in the writings of St. John. In 1 John 1:7, contrasting the assemblies of the Church to those of the

---

43 Thus the RSV renders it "participation."

heretics and schismatics,[44] John writes, "If we walk in the light as He is in the light, we have fellowship [koinonia] with one another, and the blood of Jesus Christ His Son cleanses us from all sin." That is, if we Christians walk in righteousness (unlike the heretics, who walk in unrighteousness), we can gather together on Sundays to have eucharistic koinonia one with another, and in that eucharistic fellowship, the Blood of Jesus that we receive from the chalice cleanses us from all sin.

We see this apostolic understanding of the Eucharist as sacrificial and as the Real Presence of Christ's Body and Blood in the years immediately following the witness of the apostles.

In Clement's First Letter,[45] dated to about AD 96, he wrote from Rome to the neighboring church of Corinth. Some of the presbyter-bishops had been unjustly deposed from office in a rebellion, and Clement wrote to rebuke the rebels and call everyone to peace and proper order. In chapter 44 he wrote as follows: "It will be no small sin for us if we depose from the bishop's office those who have offered [Greek *prosphero*] the gifts blamelessly and in holiness."[46] We note that the job of the liturgical leaders was to "offer the gifts," which is a sacrificial term. It was used because it was understood by all as early as the time of Clement[47] that the Eucharist is sacrificial.

The *Didache* (dated from about AD 100) also refers in chapter 14 to the Eucharist as "your sacrifice," referencing as a proof text Malachi 1:11, which reads, "In every place incense *shall be* offered to My name, / And a pure offering."[48] Again we note that the Eucharist was regarded as a sacrifice from the very beginning.

---

44   Compare 1 John 2:18–19.
45   So-called; the document known as 2 Clement is not from him.
46   *The Apostolic Fathers*, ed. Michael W. Holmes (Grand Rapids, MI: Baker Academic, 2007), 105.
47   Traditionally identified with the friend of Paul referred to in Philippians 4:3.
48   *Apostolic Fathers*, 365–367.

Further, St. Ignatius, Bishop of Antioch, who was martyred in about 107, speaks of the Eucharist repeatedly. In his Letter to the Ephesians he warns against heretics and schismatics, reminding his hearers that "if anyone is not within the sanctuary, he lacks the bread of God"[49]—the sanctuary being a reference to the temple and the Church, the place of sacrifice. The Church was a sanctuary because in it the sacrifice of the Eucharist was offered.

Ignatius also referred to the Eucharist as "the medicine of immortality, the antidote we take in order not to die but to live forever in Jesus Christ."[50] For Ignatius, the Eucharist was no mere visual reminder but a saving medicine.

In his Letter to the Philadelphians, he exhorted them, "Take care to participate in one Eucharist, for there is one flesh of our Lord Jesus Christ, and one cup that leads to unity through His Blood; there is one altar, just as there is one bishop."[51] Again we see the identification of the bread and cup with the Lord's Body and Blood.

In his Letter to the Smyrnaeans, Ignatius again warns of the heretics and describes them as those who "abstain from Eucharist and prayer because they refuse to acknowledge that the Eucharist is the flesh of our Savior Jesus Christ, which suffered for our sins and which the Father by His goodness raised up."[52] Again we see that the Eucharist not only represents the Savior's flesh; it "*is* the flesh of our Savior."

The witness of Ignatius, whose ministry was mostly in the apostolic first century in a city as foundational to the Faith as Antioch, is tremendously important, for it allows us to see how the Church regarded the Eucharist as the first century gave way to the second. Ignatius clearly believed that the Eucharist is

---

49 *Apostolic Fathers*, 187.
50 *Apostolic Fathers*, 199.
51 *Apostolic Fathers*, 239.
52 *Apostolic Fathers*, 255.

sacrificial, that it is the true Flesh and Blood of Christ, and that it is through the Eucharist that the faithful receive eternal life.

We have already seen how Justin Martyr (d. ca. 165) asserted that "not as common bread and common drink do we receive these" but that the Eucharist "is the flesh and blood of Jesus who was made flesh" (*Apology*, ch. 66).[53] Note once again: not "represents" or "symbolizes," but "*is*."

Irenaeus (d. ca. 202) wrote about the Eucharist of the Church in his massive multivolume work *Against Heresies*. He regarded the Eucharist as a sacrifice and the cup as containing the Lord's Blood. Thus he wrote that Jesus "took that created thing, bread, and gave thanks, and said, 'This is My Body.' And the cup likewise, which is part of that creation to which we belong He confessed to be His Blood, and taught the new sacrifice of the new covenant, which the Church receiving from the apostles offers to God throughout the world" (4.17.5).[54]

Irenaeus also wrote, "We offer to Him His own, announcing consistently the fellowship and union of the flesh and Spirit. For as the bread, which is produced from the earth, when it receives the invocation of God, is no longer common bread, but the Eucharist, consisting of two realities, earthly and heavenly, so also our bodies, when they receive the Eucharist, are no longer corruptible, having the hope of the resurrection to eternity" (4.18.5).[55]

Again we see the same teaching as found in Ignatius decades earlier: the Eucharist is a sacrifice, the true Body and Blood of Christ, through which we find eternal life.

There is therefore an identity of teaching between the New Testament and the earliest Fathers—an identity that witnesses to the Church's faithful preservation of the apostolic Tradition regarding the Eucharist. This early patristic understanding of

53 Ante-Nicene Fathers, vol. 1, 185.
54 Ante-Nicene Fathers, vol. 1, 484.
55 Ante-Nicene Fathers, vol. 1, 486.

the Eucharist was so widespread and unanimous in the second-century Church because it was the teaching that all the churches received from the apostles. It is this tradition the Orthodox Church continues to preserve to this day.

CHAPTER NINE

Open or Closed—or Organic?

Communion

Many Evangelicals visiting Orthodox churches are surprised and (though they are polite about it) often somewhat offended that they cannot receive Holy Communion there. In their experience and understanding, the reception of Communion is open to all. This is sometimes called "open Communion" and is contrasted to "closed Communion," which limits the reception of Holy Communion to those of a given group.

The practice of open Communion is rooted in the evangelical understanding of what Holy Communion is and does—namely, that it is an occasional and precious devotional reminder that Christ died for them, a time to rededicate themselves to the Savior. It is an intensely personal and individual thing—Jesus died for me, and so I express my gratitude to Him for that saving death and the salvation it brought me. The Orthodox refusal to commune the non-Orthodox looks and, more significantly, feels as though the Orthodox are denying that the non-Orthodox are saved. If one is saved, one may receive Communion in an evangelical church,[56] and so the refusal to commune is regarded as

---

56 There are, of course, exceptions. Some Reformed groups practice a form of closed Communion, and some Baptistic groups only commune those who have been baptized as adults.

declaring that all non-Orthodox are not saved. Since the Orthodox Church does not in fact regard non-Orthodox as unsaved,
why do they deny them Holy Communion?

In sorting all this out, we must first look again at why the
Church has always refused to commune non-Orthodox or those
in schism. The Orthodox Church's practice is rooted in what they
believe the Eucharist accomplishes. The classic statement is found
in St. Paul's words in 1 Corinthians 10:17: "For we, *though* many,
are one bread *and* one body; for we all partake of that one bread."
That is, when the many faithful each partake of the one eucharistic bread, they are reconstituted as one body in the Church. In
this spiritual symbiosis, the Church makes the Eucharist and the
Eucharist makes the Church. Thus the Eucharist not only brings
the transforming and healing grace of God to the individual who
partakes of it, but it also unites that individual to other individuals in the one Body of Christ. In this sacrament one cannot separate Christ from His Church: the Eucharist unites one to Christ
because it unites one to His Body, the Church. The Church is not
merely a gathered group of individuals. When the Christians
gather, Christ is in their midst to such an extent that *the Church
is Christ.*

We see this in Paul's vocabulary. For example, in 1 Corinthians 12:12, he speaks of the various members of a human body
all constituting one single body, and when he applies this reality to the Corinthian church, he does not say, "so also *is the
Church,*" though this is what he means. Instead he says, "so also
is Christ"—identifying the Church with Christ. He says the same
thing in Ephesians 1:23, where he writes that the Church "is His
body, the fullness of Him who fills all in all." The Eucharist unites
those who partake of it to Christ *because it unites them to His
Church,* reincorporating them as fellow members of that Body. In
the Eucharist we are joined not only to Christ but also to all the
other members of His Body.

We further ask: What does it mean to belong to a body? Membership in any body—not just the Christian Church, but any corporate reality—involves two things: unity of faith or ideology and commitment to mutual discipline. Take, for example, something very different from the Christian Church, such as the Communist Party. To become and remain a member in this body, one must subscribe to certain tenets (i.e., those of communism) and abide by its mutual discipline. Thus if one rejected the tenets of communism or if one profited from certain business enterprises, thereby rejecting the party's insistence that one forgo private property, one would quite properly be rejected for membership in the Communist Party. To be a part of a body that defines itself over against those not a part of that body, one must subscribe to its common tenets or faith and live consistently with those tenets. That is what it means to be part of a body and not an outsider.

It is the same with the body of the Christian Church: to be a part of the Church one must subscribe to its tenets (i.e., to the Orthodox Faith) and live consistently with those tenets. If one does not hold to that Faith or if one refuses to be bound by the lifestyle it demands, one cannot be a part of that body. Baptists, for example, do not subscribe to the Orthodox Faith (if you doubt this, go into any Baptist Church and begin to offer prayer to the Theotokos), and they do not regard themselves as bound to the disciplines that define and bind the Orthodox. Wonderful as Baptists are, they cannot be a part of the Orthodox Church— not because the Orthodox are mean or exclusionary but because the Baptists cannot fulfill the requirements of what it means to belong to the body of the Orthodox Church.

We now can see why the Church from its inception has steadfastly refused to commune those who are outside it. If one cannot properly belong to the Church because one cannot confess the Church's Faith or accept the Church's moral discipline, one cannot be communed, because communing would unite one to a body to which one cannot properly belong. Receiving the Eucharist unites one to the body that celebrates it, and the heretic or schismatic (to give their classical names) rejects the conditions required for membership in that body. The very nature of the Church forbids such Communion. It not only would give no benefit to the outsider communed (and might actually do them harm; see 1 Cor. 11:27f), but it also harms the Church itself, for it would thereby admit alien influences into it, like leaven into a lump.

Evangelicals, of course, do not share this view of the Eucharist. For them reception of Communion is entirely an individual matter and lacks the corporate aspect of uniting them to other communicants in one body. They are quite consistent in offering Communion to Christians of other denominations, since all partaking in Communion does, in their view, is to express gratitude to God for Christ's death on the Cross. Since Christians from other denominations can share their gratitude for the death of Christ, there is no reason they cannot also share their Communion.

It is hard to fault their consistency. Given this theology, they would indeed be narrow, churlish, and wrong to deny Communion to those in other denominations. But Orthodoxy has a different eucharistic theology, and in this theology confining reception of Holy Communion to the members of the Orthodox family does not mean that Communion is "closed" to others but that it is organic—that Communion unites the communicant to the living body and the fullness of the Church. Holy Communion not only expresses gratitude for the death of Christ on the Cross; it also unites believers to other believers in the one body. The legitimacy of open Communion depends on an individualistic understanding of the Eucharist—an understanding foreign to the Orthodox Church.

CHAPTER TEN

"No graven image"

Pictures of Christ and the Saints

Evangelical churches have inherited from the Reformation the Protestant hostility to Catholic imagery, especially statues, which were intimately linked to Marian devotion and devotion to the saints. That is why, although such statues find no place in classic Protestant churches, other forms of imagery are allowed, such as images of Christ and His saints in stained glass windows and pictures of Jesus in the Sunday school and in children's Bibles. The real issue is not so much a total ban on religious imagery as it is a ban on imagery associated with Catholic devotion.

Having accepted a "back to the Bible" approach to worship, however, it becomes necessary to back up this hostility to Catholic images with Bible verses. The Ten Commandments, being part of the Mosaic hostility to pagan religion, provide plenty of such verses.

In Exodus 20:4–5 (KJV), we read the following divine prohibition:

Thou shalt not make unto thee any graven image, or any likeness of any thing that is in heaven above, or that is in the earth beneath, or that is in the water under the earth. Thou shalt not bow down thyself to them, nor serve them: for I the LORD thy God am a jealous God, visiting the iniquity of the fathers upon the children unto the third and fourth generation of them that hate me.

This commandment does not merely prohibit the worship of pagan gods (that was already prohibited in the First Commandment in v. 3) but the use of pagan-inspired statuary ("graven" or carved images) to represent Yahweh. Pagan gods could be and were represented with (for example) a god having the head of a falcon, but no such image was allowed to represent Yahweh. The pagan gods might be the embodiments of the forces of nature and thus fitly represented by creatures such as falcons or bull calves, but not Israel's God. He was above His creation and utterly transcendent. The use of any such image could only serve to denigrate His nature, reducing Him to the level of the pagan gods.

This is clear from Deuteronomy 4:12—when God revealed Himself to Israel on Mount Sinai and spoke from the midst of the fire, the people "saw no form—only a voice." Therefore no form of Yahweh was allowed to Israel. He could not be portrayed in human or animal form, as the other gods were. In His shrine, the Holy of Holies, there stood no statue such as could be found in the shrines of the pagan gods—only the ark of the covenant, witnessing to His invisible presence.[57] Based on texts like these,

---

57   Some evangelical scholars such as J. I. Packer have further argued that *any* use of image to depict Christ inevitably (and sinfully) limits Him, since a single image cannot reveal the entire truth about Him. That is true, but it ignores the fact that a single image never claims to reveal all that could be revealed—nor could a single Bible verse or a single sermon. A single image, Bible verse, or sermon is only ever intended to reveal one aspect of the total truth and form one note in a larger symphony of revelation. In this sense, all images, verses, and sermons are symbolic in that they cannot reveal the totality of truth, which always remains larger than any single representation.

Evangelicals have been keen to ban all imagery of Christ and His saints from their public worship, although they usually turn a blind eye to pictures of Christ in children's materials or to images on stained glass windows.

In contrast, Orthodox churches are full of images—not "graven" or carved images or statuary such as fill Catholic churches in the West, but flat two-dimensional images, "icons," pictures created with paint or mosaic. (Evangelicals also apply the Pentateuchal ban on carved statues to such icons, since the engine driving the ban is not biblical literalism but historical hostility to Catholic devotion to the saints—a devotion found also in Orthodoxy.)

In the long history of the Church, a movement known as iconoclasm arose in the eighth century which objected to the painting, decorative use, and veneration of icons. Reacting to this movement allowed the Church to reflect more fully on why it has always accepted the principle of Christian art and why it has always used icons.

Anti-iconoclastic writers such as St. John of Damascus have noted that the Mosaic ban on images was never absolute.[58] Though banning the use of an image of "any likeness of any thing that is in heaven above," God still commanded that carved images of the heavenly cherubim be made and fastened to the ark. A closer look at the Pentateuch reveals that the intention was always to ban a syncretistic approach to worship that resulted in the creation of cult statues or images of Yahweh comparable to the cult statues or images of the pagan gods.

Anti-iconoclastic writers also noted the reason for the

---

58 Nor was the ban rigorously enforced in later Judaism: the synagogue in Dura-Europos on the banks of the Euphrates has its western wall abundantly adorned with images of Moses, David, and Elijah. Though it is not typical of Jewish synagogues, its witness against rigorism is still important.

ban—namely that not only was Yahweh superior to the gods and should not be diminished by comparing Him to the forces of nature ("swift as a falcon, strong as a bull calf"), but Yahweh was invisible and could not be seen. Though He could appear in a vision or theophany, His true form remained invisible, which is why Israel did not see Him through the fire of Mount Sinai. This underwent a dramatic change with the Incarnation. At that time, the invisible God became visible when He united human nature to Himself in the womb of the Virgin. After Christ's Birth and growth to manhood, the previously undepictable God had become depictable. Christ is therefore the image (Greek *eikon*, "icon") of the invisible God (Col. 1:15). In Him the invisible God had become visible.

The prohibitions in the Pentateuch served God's purpose in their day in that they taught Israel about the transcendence of the divine nature. Those prohibitions, like the rest of the Law, acted as a disciplinarian to bring Israel to Christ (Gal. 3:23–25). Now that Christ has come, we are no longer under that disciplinarian, and the prohibitions about imagery no longer apply. The prohibitions were meant to forbid Israel from limiting their God. But God can voluntarily limit Himself in the Incarnation. Since He has done so, He can now be depicted in an image.

Obviously a single religious image cannot reveal all that can be revealed about Christ, but that is the nature of *all* imagery— no single image, photo, or portrait can reveal everything about *any* human being. No one supposes that such total revelation is a function of imagery. Any image, be it of Christ or of any person, is essentially symbolic: one looks at it and identifies the image with the prototype regardless of such ontological asymmetry. A painted portrait or statue of Abraham Lincoln, for example, functions as a true representation of Lincoln even though it may not be a photographic double of him and cannot reveal everything about him. Thus to spit on the image of Lincoln is to show disrespect for Lincoln himself. The honor (or dishonor) done to the image passes to its prototype.

The Church has always had images of Christ. While the Church was poor and persecuted and survived by flying under the Roman radar, obviously whatever images it could afford could not be openly and unambiguously displayed. Accordingly we find such images in funerary art, and even there they are highly symbolic. For example, Christ is portrayed as a shepherd—pagan viewers would see only a shepherd, while Christian viewers would see the Good Shepherd, Jesus the Savior of the sheep. In images of Mary, pagans would see only a woman, while Christians would see the Mother of the Incarnate God.

This hiddenness and ambiguity could come to an end after the Christians emerged from the cultural catacombs and public buildings set aside for Christian worship came to be built. Then the Christian acceptance and appreciation of art and images could find full expression, and churches became adorned with images of the Savior and His saints.

After the iconoclastic challenge to the Church's immemorial use of icons, Christian writers reflected more fully on their rationale and their devotional use. Icons could be used not only as adornments of church buildings but also to express honor and love for Christ and His saints, and so individual, smaller icons on boards multiplied. If one could express one's love for Christ by kissing the Gospel book and the cross (as even the iconoclasts admitted was acceptable), then why not also use icons for that purpose? With icons, as with the Gospel book and the cross, the honor shown to the image passes to the prototype.[59]

---

59   This is immediately recognized in other contexts. When the Communists desecrated the icons by shooting out their eyes and by urinating on them, it was understood that the dishonor was intended not for the icons but for Christ and His saints. Also, when one kisses a photo of someone loved and cherished, it is understood

For these reasons the Orthodox Church makes full use of icons. Though their use is not mandatory, it is the natural fruit of love and devotion to Christ and His saints, and it is exceedingly rare to find an Orthodox Church without at least a few icons. We show our worship of Christ and our love for His Mother and His saints through acts of devotion to their images.[60]

---

that the devotion is intended for the person in the photo, not for the photo itself.

60 Obviously our devotion to Christ is absolute, while our devotion to His Mother and His saints is of a lesser kind, since Christ alone is God. This difference of devotion is centered in the unseen heart and is typically expressed as the difference between *latria* (or worship) given to Christ and *dulia* (or honor) given to His saints.

CHAPTER ELEVEN

"He who believes and is baptized"

The Baptism of Infants

Evangelicals do not believe that baptism regenerates the penitent soul or that it bestows the remission of sins, but they do consider it to be important. In their view, regeneration, remission of sins, and salvation are accomplished through conversion and saying the sinner's prayer, asking Jesus into the heart. Baptism—always by immersion, usually single[61]—is regarded as the public testimony and witness to this prior work of grace. Because it follows a conversion experience, it can only be administered to those who have had the experience—that is, people old enough to voluntarily and sincerely ask Jesus into their heart. That of course excludes infants and very young children. The rite of baptism is usually referred to as "believer's baptism" to differentiate it from infant baptism.

Evangelicals believe that baptism administered to infants and young children prior to their conversion experience is no real baptism at all. It does not "count"—it is at best regarded as a kind of watery dedication. (Most Evangelicals will dedicate

---

61 This contrasts to the invariable and universal practice of the early Church, which knew only of a triple immersion, one for each of the three Trinitarian Names.

their children to God apart from baptism.[62]) Accordingly, people baptized in their infancy are encouraged to be (re)baptized after their adult conversion. One sometimes hears of cases of people receiving such adult baptism multiple times as they repeatedly rededicate themselves to God at various times in their life, but this repeated use of adult baptism is unusual and frowned upon.

The rejection of infant baptism began at the Reformation, with some more radical groups (such as early Mennonites) insisting that baptism could only be administered to those confessing adult faith. (Such early "anabaptists" were less insistent on total immersion.) In societies where infant baptism was effectively divorced from fervent faith and tended to function more as a rite for legitimating children as proper citizens, one can feel some sympathy for their protest. The early Anabaptists insisted that church gatherings must consist only of people who had had a conversion experience, as opposed to the model found among Catholics, Lutherans, and Calvinists, who insisted that everyone in society was a part of the Church. The Anabaptists' different understanding of baptism was thus rooted in a different ecclesiology and understanding of the relationship between Church and society.

Naturally proof texts were sought from Scripture to support this understanding of baptism. We cite a few of them.

Mark 16:16 preserves a saying of Christ that in response to the Church's preaching of the gospel, "He who believes and is baptized will be saved; but he who does not believe will be condemned." Our Lord's own preaching had been summarized as "The time is fulfilled, and the kingdom of God is at hand. Repent, and believe in the gospel" (Mark 1:15). From these citations it was concluded that one must repent and believe before one could be baptized; since infants could neither repent nor believe, they

---

62 Biblical support is often sought in the dedication of Samuel to God (in 1 Sam. 1), despite the fact that this dedication was entirely unique.

should not be baptized. Examples were also cited from the Acts of the Apostles, in which all the conversions reported were of adults (though the complete absence of infants and children could not be proven from the silence). Much was made of the entire absence of specific mention of infant baptism in the Gospel narratives and the Acts of the Apostles. Further, the many exhortations in the New Testament urging repentance (e.g., Acts 17:30) are interpreted as meaning that such repentance must precede baptism for baptism to be valid and effective.

By contrast, Orthodoxy takes for granted that the infant children of believers may be baptized. From both the New Testament material and the practice of the early Church, it is clear that baptism was primarily a rite applied to adult converts, who formed the overwhelming majority of those joining the Church. But since it involved the power of God coming upon the baptized and was not simply a human act of witness, the rite was also administered to the infant children of Christian adults, for God's power could work within infants as well as adults (as proven by John the Baptizer receiving the Holy Spirit while yet in his mother's womb; Luke 1:15).

The inclusion of infants among the baptized is rooted in the pre-Christian history of the rite. Christian baptism was modeled on John's baptism as the means of becoming a disciple of Christ, and John's baptism in turn grew out of Jewish proselyte baptism. Proselyte baptism was the means by which a Gentile convert became a Jew. A Gentile man wanting to convert would approach the local Jewish community and express his desire. He and all the males of his household would be circumcised, and after they had healed, all in the house would be dipped in water or baptized to wash away the ceremonial impurity of the Gentile world. After that, those baptized were considered Jews. And included in the baptism of the household were women *and infants*.

It is likely, therefore, that households coming to John for

baptism would have been baptized in their entirety, including infants and young children. Since that was the model of household baptism that John received from proselyte baptism and that Christ received from John, it is quite likely that households coming to Christ for baptism would have been baptized in their entirety too, including infants. So when Paul later baptized an entire household (Acts 16:31), that would have included any infants in the household.

The New Testament does not mention such infants, because it was not given to us as a rule book covering every possible situation or exigency. And since it is a series of letters dating from the first Christian generation, certain questions would not yet have arisen. Rather, the New Testament presupposes a largely adult audience, and that is why it is replete with exhortations to repent. It is not answering the question, "What is always needed for baptism?" but the more general question, "What should unbaptized pagan adults do?" The answer: Repent and believe.

But that said, and consistently with the practice of household baptism, Paul did occasionally address households inclusively, giving directions to children just as he did to their parents (e.g., Eph. 6:1–4). In his letter to the Corinthians about the legitimacy of mixed marriages of a Christian to a non-Christian, he refers to the children of such marriages as "holy" (1 Cor. 7:14), which at least suggests that he included them in some way within the household of faith. There is no suggestion that the infants and young children of baptized adult converts would have been excluded from the Christian Church.

The proof of the apostolic precedent for infant baptism, however, is found in the history and praxis of the earliest Church. If the apostles had left a clear precedent against infant baptism and disallowed it, in contrast to proselyte household baptism, the practice of infant baptism would have created some controversy and left its mark on church history. In fact, no such controversy is recorded. On the contrary, infant baptism was assumed to be of apostolic provenance.[63]

We first look at the witness of Origen, the Church's first (and controversial) systematic theologian, who flourished in Alexandria and Palestine and who died in 254. He clearly knew of infant baptism and approved of it. In one of his sermons on Luke's Gospel, he says,

> Little children are baptized "for the remission of sins." ... Yet how can this explanation of the baptismal washing be maintained in the case of small children, except according to the interpretation we spoke of earlier? "No man is clean of stain, not even if his life upon the earth had lasted but a single day." ... For this reason, even small children are baptized.

We may or may not agree with Origen about the rationale for baptizing infants, but there is no doubt that the Church of his day did indeed baptize them. And this practice was not new in his day. Origen writes, "the church had a tradition from the apostles to give baptism even to infants" (from his *Commentary on the Epistle to the Romans*). Therefore, the practice of infant baptism at the very least went back beyond living memory in Origen's day, and this places it very early indeed.

We also look at the document known as *The Apostolic Tradition*, ascribed to Hippolytus of Rome (d. 235), which represents the practice of its day. And this practice took for granted (1) that most baptisms were of converts, and (2) that small children could also be baptized. The relevant bit from the document reads, "First

---

63 The protest of Tertullian of North Africa (d. c. 220) is the exception that proves the rule. Though resisting the practice because he felt that sin committed after baptism was all but unforgivable, he did not dispute the antiquity of the practice. Tertullian was resisting not an innovation but a long-standing custom.

baptize the small children. And each one who is able to speak for themselves, let them speak. But those not able to speak for themselves, let their parents or another one belonging to their family speak for them. Afterward baptize the grown men, and finally, the women" (*Apostolic Tradition*, ch. 21). Here we see that the small child's inability to speak for itself was not a problem; the parents or sponsors simply gave the responses (just as they do in Orthodox baptisms today).

We also look at the witness of St. Cyprian of Carthage (d. 258). A fellow bishop of his named Fidus knew that infants were baptized but thought perhaps the baptism should be deferred until the eighth day of the infant's life, by analogy with Jewish circumcision—perhaps because St. Paul called baptism "the circumcision of Christ" in Colossians 2:11. Cyprian met with sixty-six of his fellow North African bishops in council and considered Fidus's suggestion of waiting until the eighth day to baptize infants. Cyprian and the council unanimously rejected the suggestion, saying that the infant should be baptized immediately after birth, on the second or third day. This indicates a well-established practice in North Africa—so well established in fact that the only debate was whether to baptize the baby right after birth or to wait for eight days. Practices of and rationale for the baptism of infants varied from place to place (especially in the East), but no one denied that it could be done.

The earliest practice of the Church therefore witnesses to the apostolic provenance for the baptism of infants. Through baptism the seed and regenerating power of God is placed within the young child, to be nurtured by the Christian parents as the child grows and eventually owns and confesses the Faith for himself. This means, of course, that infant baptism should be administered only to the children of devout parents, those with fervent faith who will take care to raise the child to their own level of commitment to Christ.

CHAPTER TWELVE

"Worship the Lord in holy array"

The Use of Church Vestments

Evangelical clergy do not don any vestments or special clothing before performing their services, though occasionally the
choir will perform dressed in choir robes. There seems to be no
theological reason for officiating in normal streetwear (which may
consist of anything from casual clothing to a three-piece suit).
It seems that because Catholic clergy (and their Protestant step-
children, such as the Anglicans) use clergy vestments, Evangelicals
choose not to.

The Orthodox custom of dressing all the officiants, from the
clergy to the altar boys, in special church vestments forms a
marked contrast. The use of special vestments for church services represents a departure from the custom of the early Church.
Though the priests of the Jewish temple wore special vestments
when serving at the altar, the original Christian clergy (the apostles and presbyters) did not. They came to the Christian assembly and prayed there in their ordinary clothes. Given the importance of the eucharistic assembly, no doubt they came in the best
clothes they had (the emperor Julian the Apostate tried to mock
them by pointing out how they dressed up to worship God), but
those clothes would have been worn at special non-church occa-
sions as well.

The average bishop in those pre-Nicene days, and even afterward, wore the clothing of any upper-class gentleman: a linen robe with close sleeves called a *linea*, covering the whole body from neck to feet, a *tunica* with short sleeves over that, and then over both of them a *paenula*, a large round piece of clothing with a hole in the center for the head to pass through, which fell in folds over the shoulders and arms and draped the body down to the knees. As Dom Gregory Dix points out (in his *The Shape of the Liturgy*), this was what Bishop Cyprian was wearing in 258 when he was martyred. As history records, when he arrived at the place of his martyrdom, Cyprian took off his *paenula*, folded it up, knelt down on it, and prayed. He then took off his *tunica*, handed it to his deacons, and stood up in his *linea* to await execution. Later generations might look back to the martyr and his clothing and conclude that he was wearing a *phelonion,* which he folded, and finally stood up in his *sticharion*—the special vestments he wore only when serving Liturgy. In fact, he was wearing the normal outdoor clothing that any Roman gentleman wore.

What happened, of course, is that clothing styles in the world changed as the clothing worn by the new barbarians became fashionable. The Church, however, conservative as ever, kept the fashion that had been used in antiquity. When Emperor Constantine donated to the cathedral church at Jerusalem "a sacred robe" of gold tissue to be worn by the bishop when presiding at Paschal baptisms, he was simply donating a very fancy piece of clothing— the ancient equivalent of an Armani suit.

Far from the clergy always vesting in special clothes when they presided at worship, the introduction of special clothes was greeted with opposition and some hostility. The first vestment to be used especially in church was a scarf, usually made of colored silk. As Dix wrote, "This was the old 'scarf of office' worn by the emperor and consuls, a badge granted to numerous other officials during the fourth century. It was adopted by the clergy in various forms. . . . For the lower clergy it becomes the 'stole' worn in different ways by bishops, priests, and deacons as a badge of distinction." Bishops wore it in one way (now seen in the modern episcopal *omophorion*), priests in another way (the modern stole), and deacons yet another way (the *orarion* worn over the left shoulder). The clergy in those days wore it as a mark of distinction.

But as stated above, not everyone in those early days approved of it. An early bishop of Rome in about 425, Celestine, emphatically did *not* approve. He learned that some bishops in Gaul (modern France) were adopting this fashion, and he wrote to rebuke them in no uncertain terms:

> It is small wonder that the church's custom should be violated by those who have not grown old in the church, but entering in by some other way have introduced into the church along with themselves things which they used to wear in another way of life [i.e., when they were civil magistrates]. Whence came this custom in the churches of Gaul, so contrary to antiquity? We bishops must be distinguished from the people and others by our learning, not by our dress, by our life, not by our robes, by purity of heart, not by elegance.

One can sympathize with the papal point of view: the true adornment is internal, not external. Pomp and frippery, the pope said, have no place in the church, for such externals can overwhelm the internal, stealing focus from where it belongs. However, eventually all the churches, West and East, came to use special vestments while serving Liturgy, and now the sight of clergy serving in a nice secular suit in a liturgical church would be spectacularly jarring.

Though the development from secular dress to liturgical vestments may have been gradual and in some ways unintentional, it has been the custom of the Church for about a thousand years. The question may be asked: Since the custom is not apostolic (as Pope Celestine pointedly reminded his northern colleagues), could or should we change it? If St. John Chrysostom served Liturgy in the equivalent of a nice Armani suit (or knowing Chrysostom's disdain for pomp at the capital, more probably a nice sport coat from Walmart), why cannot Orthodox clergy today serve the Liturgy of St. John Chrysostom in secular clothing? It would certainly serve to put the main focus on the internal person of the heart rather than on dress, robes, or elegance.

The problem with changing the current custom by returning to an older one is that history has no reset button, no rewind switch. In a word, *changing* from church vestments to secular clothes is not the same thing as *retaining* secular clothes. That is because there is more at stake in this change than simply the kind of clothes on one's back. Clothing, like everything else in history, tends to accumulate significance, and the fact that the accumulation is accidental and unintended is irrelevant. Like it or not, the change of custom regarding vestments now involves more than merely choice of dress. Like every other cultural artifact, vestments accumulated significance as time progressed. Vestments now all come invisibly laden with history and therefore with hidden and perhaps unacknowledged approaches to Christian life and spirituality. They therefore bring with them the world and entire theological approach of the historical Orthodox Church.

Thus, *jettisoning* vestments is not at all the same thing as *not having* vestments in the first place. Getting rid of vestments today would involve jettisoning something we have and would thus be making an important statement about more than simply vestments. We Orthodox would be making a statement about and rejecting many things in our tradition that are now expressed by our use of vestments. If we would retain these precious things in Tradition—such as the solemnity of worship, the sacrificial and sacramental nature of the Eucharist, and the authority of clergy in parish life—vestments are here to stay.

CONCLUSION

Converting to Orthodoxy

An Interior Revolution

Evangelicals and Orthodox, as we have seen, differ in many basic beliefs and practices, even as they agree in many others. Naturally, since each believes their doctrine to be true, each wants those who differ from them to agree with them: Evangelicals want Orthodox to become Evangelicals, and Orthodox want Evangelicals to become Orthodox. That does not make either group intolerant or theologically imperialistic. It only makes them consistent with their theology—naturally, every Christian group should prefer truth to error when it comes to doctrine.

There is, however, one more thing that differentiates Orthodoxy from Evangelicalism, and that is Orthodoxy's ecclesiology. Evangelicals generally believe that in converting from Orthodoxy to, for example, Pentecostalism, the devout Orthodox is exchanging doctrinal error for doctrinal truth and is moving from one Christian denomination to another (assuming of course that the devout Orthodox was truly converted to Christ before leaving Orthodoxy). It is otherwise with the Orthodox: they believe that in converting from Pentecostalism to Orthodoxy, one is not simply exchanging doctrinal error for doctrinal truth or moving from one denomination to another, but leaving schism to join the original, one, holy, catholic, and apostolic Church. Protestantism regards "the Church" as the conglomeration of all truly born-again Christians from all Trinitarian denominations. Therefore, a born-again Christian moving from, say, the Baptist Church to the Alliance Church is still staying within the Church.

This is not the ecclesiology of the Fathers or of the Orthodox. For the Fathers and for their Orthodox heirs, substantial divergence from the Faith of the Church constitutes heresy, and groups that had the integrity and honesty to split from the original apostolic Church on the basis of this divergence and go into schism (defining themselves as rival bodies from this original group) were no longer regarded as part of the Church. In His final high-priestly prayer recorded in John 17, our Lord asked the Father that His disciples would remain one, united to one another in the same unity that united Him to the Father. This prayer was immediately fulfilled; it does not refer to a future reunion of all the denominations, for when Christ prayed this prayer, those denominations did not exist. Rather, the prayer referred to the unbreakable unity that was bestowed on the Church on the Day of Pentecost.

This means that Christ's Church forever remains one Church, with its members united to one another and to God. It is incapable of substantial division, for it maintains the unity for which Christ prayed. Substantial division of His Church is therefore impossible: a group or individual could split *from* the Church, but the Church itself could not be split or divided. In the early Church, heresy and the consequent establishment of a rival altar constituted not a split *within* the Church but the setting up of a group *apart from* the Church. This is what is meant in the Creed by the confession that we believe in "one, holy, catholic, and apostolic Church": the Church cannot lose its holiness, or its catholicity, or its apostolicity and still remain Christ's Church. Neither can it lose its essential unity; by creedal definition the Church remains one. This was the emphatic teaching of every Church

Father; there was no dissenting voice within Christian antiquity regarding the Church's unity.

Then came our modern period, with its assertion that schism and separation from the historical Church did *not* possess the same significance assigned to it by the Fathers. Given the problems afflicting the Western church in the medieval period following its schism from the Orthodox East, one understands the insistence of the Protestant Reformers that separation from the papal West was imperative. The early Reformers regarded the pope as the eschatological antichrist, and this could not help but make schism from the papal church an urgent necessity. Nonetheless, the ultimate result was the acceptance of schism as a defining feature of the Protestant churches. That is, schism from the papal church was accepted as normal and necessary, for the papal church (they thought) was not the true Church but Babylon the Great, the mother of harlots and the abominations of the earth (Rev. 17:5). For them the choice seemed to be either schism or apostasy.

Protestantism thus gradually came to lose the primitive Christian horror of schism. As time went on, with the continuing multiplication of Protestant denominations, what came to matter among them was purity of doctrine, not unity—and sometimes doctrine took a back seat to lesser things. The concept of schism has all but vanished from the theological glossary of Evangelicals: if one doesn't like one's church, one simply leaves and starts another one down the street. What the Fathers decried as schism is now regarded as normal church growth. So long as the new church does not make a point of denying the Trinity, it remains a part of the *una sancta*, the one holy Church.

This minimalistic view of ecclesiological unity has little in common with the approach of the Fathers, who insisted on a substantial unity of both faith and practice in local communities before they could be accepted as part of the *una sancta*, the one, holy, catholic, and apostolic Church. For the Fathers, substantial divergence in matters of faith separated a community from the body of the one Church, with the result that the members of that community were no longer in communion with the rest of the Church. Restoration to the unity of the Church depended on the divergent body's renunciation of its error and its return to catholic unity of faith and practice. Otherwise it remained in schism, standing outside the unity of the one Church.

This understanding of ecclesiological unity remains normative in Orthodoxy today. Orthodoxy regards the Protestant denominations (and, come to that, our Roman Catholic friends as well) as being in schism from the one, united, and indivisible Church. The root ecumenical problem therefore is not simply difference of doctrine but schism. The Orthodox believe that they are the one, holy, catholic, and apostolic Church confessed in the Creed. Converts to Orthodoxy are invited not only to agree with its teaching but to join its family. In converting to Orthodoxy, they are not simply joining a different denomination but returning from schism.

It should hardly need stating that all this does not mean that the Orthodox are better than others, or that there is no grace or salvation to be found outside the Church's borders, or that the Orthodox have nothing to learn from other Christians. To err is human, and there is more than enough humanity in Orthodoxy to go around. The issue here is not one of merit but solely of the nature of the Church and of its unity.

This, I suggest, is the fundamental task of those converting to Orthodoxy and the necessary interior revolution they are called to undergo: to realize that they are not simply leaving one denomination to join another one but rather leaving schism to enter the one true Church. As said above, that does not mean that the group they left had no saving grace or value. But it does mean that the group was in schism and that Christians ought to unite themselves to the original Church that Christ founded.

For whatever the value of the other Christian groups, the Lord has promised to guide and protect His Church; He made no similar promise to guide groups separated from it. The Orthodox Church, for all its faults (and they are many), abides under that protection. For conversion to Orthodoxy to be complete, the convert must understand that he or she is coming home.

The Doctrine of Eternal Security

The doctrine of eternal security is sometimes known by the tag "once saved, always saved." The main idea is that salvation by its very nature changes a person so much that apostasy becomes an existential impossibility. But then, one does ask, what about the cases of people who had been saved (i.e., who "said the sinner's prayer" and "asked Jesus into their heart") and then subsequently fell away and stopped believing in Christ or acting like a Christian? Replies come in two forms.

One form argues that such a person could not have been a "real" Christian in the first place and that there was something fundamentally flawed about her supposed experience of salvation. The other form insists that the apostate and unrepentant sinner will still be saved on the Last Day even if he committed and persisted in grievous sins such as murder or adultery. He would, however, "lose his reward." The former reply is a brilliant example of circular reasoning, and so it can never be crudely proven wrong. It does, however, mean that no real existential and subjective assurance is possible, for presumably the lapsed apostate at one time felt as sure that he had been eternally and securely saved as anyone else. The latter reply is not only wrong but dangerous and demonic, for it gives to those in danger of damnation a false sense of security.

Where do Evangelicals get this idea of eternal security? Not from the Bible, but from John Calvin. In its earlier version it went by the name "the perseverance of the saints." It formed part of the larger and more comprehensive Reformed doctrines of mankind, the Fall, and the nature of grace and salvation. Students of Calvin will recognize it as part of the famous TULIP acronym, which stands for the doctrines of Total depravity, Unconditional election, Limited atonement, Irresistible grace, and the Perseverance of the saints.

The general idea of Calvin's TULIP doctrines is that man is so fallen and incapable of even beginning to repent that God has to do it all. Before time began, God chose (or elected) certain individuals to be saved and certain other individuals to be damned—the former to the praise of His grace, and the latter to the praise of His justice. Those elected to be saved were irresistibly drawn by the Spirit to repent and exercise faith in Christ, whose death on the Cross not only paid the price for salvation but also accomplished it (thus Christ died only for the elect). Having been irresistibly drawn to faith in Christ, the elect were irresistibly kept in that faith and so could not fall away. The technical term for this understanding of divine grace is *monergism*, and the idea is that God's energy is the only effecting energy involved (hence the *mono*). Man's free will contributes precisely nothing; he repents and believes because God wills it and does it all. To be fair, the Reformed do not conceive of man as an automaton, repenting and believing automatically like a machine with no decision required from himself. A good TULIP preacher will still tell his audience to repent and believe. But he will say that *if* the sinner repents and believes, it is only because he had previously been elected and was now being irresistibly drawn.

Many Evangelicals who do not buy the full Reformed package and who would balk at the notion that Christ died only for the elect still cling to the doctrine of eternal security, not realizing it is part of a larger, coherent system of thought. Saying that one cannot fall away because the experience of salvation changes one internally makes no sense, mostly because experience teaches us that it is not so.

Of course, the Scriptures teach us that as well. The New Testament is replete with warnings not to apostatize, which would not be necessary unless apostasy were really possible. I do not warn my grandchildren about the dangers of walking on the ceiling, because walking on the ceiling is not possible for them. We only warn about dangers that are real—such as apostasy. Judas Iscariot is one example that comes to mind: he certainly fell away to the point of damnation (see John 17:12; Mark 14:21), and he certainly was once saved (Matt. 19:27–28; Acts 1:17). If one of the Twelve could fall away, then anyone can. The Epistle to the Hebrews was written to warn Christians against the possibility of such drifting away and apostasy.

I suspect that the doctrine of eternal security is Evangelicalism's attempt to meet a real pastoral need—that of assuring the trembling penitent soul that all will be well. If one fears to lose salvation if one commits a sin, or takes a sideways step, or is lazy in devotions or church-going or Bible-reading, the doctrine of eternal security functions to assure that person that their salvation is not endangered by these things.

It is true that one cannot lose one's salvation as one loses one's car keys. Salvation does not gradually evaporate like morning dew. One can drift away over time, of course, but this drift involves making decisions. One *decides* to forgo prayer and to stay away from church; one *decides* to drift. I suspect that the notion of eternal security was meant to function as a cure for the classic disease of scruples. If one does not trust God's love and imagines that a deficit of devout feeling involves a loss of salvation, then eternal security serves to reassure that trembling soul that it needn't fear such a loss of feeling. It overshoots itself, of course. It *is* possible to lose one's salvation, but it takes more than simply having a bad week or feeling less enthusiastic about spiritual things than one did when first converted.

The trembling soul should not be given the false medicine of eternal security but the true medicine of the Eucharist. Salvation is not just a single experience; it is also an ongoing journey. On that journey one continually returns to God for renewal, forgiveness, and cleansing. Penitent reception of the Eucharist assures us that we will be saved if we continue along the faithful eucharistic path. It is as the eucharistic prayer itself says: those who partake receive purification of soul, the remission of sins, the communion of the Holy Spirit, the fulfillment of the Kingdom of heaven, and boldness toward God. Standing every week at the chalice, we are eternally secure.

Musical Instruments and Orthodox Worship

The first distinctly Christian worship, in the Upper Room at the time of the Last Supper, did not use musical instruments, since such instruments were never used at Passover meals nor in the synagogue services. When the eucharistic meal was held from house to house after the Day of Pentecost, this tradition continued, and worship did not include instrumental musical accompaniment. Nor were musical instruments used in worship when the Church spread into Gentile territory: the Christians met for the Eucharist in various people's houses, but they seem to have left whatever musical instruments they had at home. They prayed, chanted, and sang (compare the pagan description of our worship as involving "singing a hymn to Christ as if to a god" in the *Letter of Pliny*), but using only the human voice.

When the Christians began to build temples for worship in earnest, after the Constantinian peace of the Church, they did not change their worship, just their location. They still did not use musical instruments but continued to chant, read, and sing just as they had always done when they were worshipping in people's homes.

Moreover, musical instruments such as the flute and the cithara were routinely used at pagan sacrifices, and the Church was keen to exclude such pagan elements from its own worship. Since these instruments tended to stir up emotion, the Church also felt that their use could lead to unseemly excess. Thus we find Clement of Alexandria (d. c. 215) writing, "If people occupy their time with pipes and psalteries and choirs and dances and Egyptian clapping of hands and such disorderly frivolities, they become quite immodest and intractable" (from *The Instructor*, 2.4).

For these reasons—both the Church's continuity with its apostolic Jewish heritage and its determination to differentiate itself from paganism—musical instruments were rigorously excluded from Christian worship. This continued to be the Church's universal practice for centuries to come.

Some suggest that the Psalter offers justification for the use of musical instruments, since it bids us to praise God with trumpet sound, with lute and harp, with timbrel and dance, with strings and pipe and sounding cymbals (see, for example, Psalm 150). And did not David use a stringed instrument to accompany his psalms (see, for example, Psalm 4)?

Two or three replies are in order.

First of all, accepting such proof-texting would have us overthrow the practice of the apostles and the Church after them—East and West—for centuries. On the basis of these verses, are we really prepared to do this? Were the apostles and the early Church after them so badly misled about something as basic as how to worship? After all, they could read the Psalter as well as anyone else.

Secondly, the worship of the Church is not the worship of the temple. Temple worship took place in the open air and included the killing, skinning, and butchering of animals, the pouring out of their blood on an altar, and the burning of their carcasses so that the smoke of the sacrifice ascended on high (hence the necessity of the open air). Loud music in the open air is a different thing from music indoors.

Also, as noted above, musical instruments accompanied

animal sacrifices at pagan rituals, so their use in temple worship was not that much different in this respect. In the ancient world, instrumental music seems to have accompanied animal sacrifices all the time. This would explain both the presence of such instruments at the temple and their absence from the synagogue and from Jewish homes at Passover time—as well as their absence from the indoor services of the Church, since in these latter places, no animals were slaughtered. In short, the verses of the Psalter exulting in instrumental music in the temple have little relevance to domestic worship outside the temple.

Finally, we note that the instruments David assumed would accompany the chanting of his psalms bore little resemblance to the organs, pianos, electric guitars, and drums of today's Western church, which are quite loud. By contrast, the stringed instruments that accompanied psalmic recitation in the ancient world did not overwhelm the recitation but were gentle and quiet adornments. No real comparison can be made between ancient music and our modern music. David's use of a stringed instrument when chanting the psalms is therefore irrelevant to our modern discussion.

We conclude by asking what is the purpose of such modern loud instrumental accompaniment? The answer: to stir up emotion (no surprise to Clement of Alexandria and the other Fathers). Indeed, all good musicians are aware of how music can be used to rouse and to soothe, to quicken the heartbeat or to pacify—or, in a word, to manipulate people's emotions and responses. That is why such instruments were always used on the battlefield: the drum, the trumpet, and the bagpipe would galvanize the advancing troops, make their blood flow fast, and stir them to action. Manipulation through music works.

And that is why the Church has always felt that instrumental music has no place in its worship. Emotion should not be artificially stirred up by organs, flutes, pianos, drums, or guitars. If emotion comes, it should come as a result of the Holy Spirit working on the human heart. The Church has therefore always subordinated music to word and melody to message. It is the Word of God, the message of the gospel, that should stir the heart, not the musical noise accompanying it.

About the Author

Archpriest Lawrence Farley is the pastor of St. Herman of Alaska Orthodox Church (OCA) in Langley, BC, Canada. He received his BA from Trinity College, Toronto, and his MDiv from Wycliffe College, Toronto. A former Anglican priest, he converted to Orthodoxy in 1985 and studied for two years at St. Tikhon's Orthodox Seminary in Pennsylvania. He has published a number of books with Ancient Faith Publishing, including the Orthodox Bible Study Companion series, *Let Us Attend*, *Unquenchable Fire*, and *A Daily Calendar of Saints*.

We hope you have enjoyed and benefited from this book. Your financial support makes it possible to continue our nonprofit ministry both in print and online. Because the proceeds from our book sales only partially cover the costs of operating **Ancient Faith Publishing** and **Ancient Faith Radio**, we greatly appreciate the generosity of our readers and listeners. Donations are tax deductible and can be made at **www.ancientfaith.com.**

To view our other publications,
please visit our website: **store.ancientfaith.com**

Bringing you Orthodox Christian music, readings, prayers, teaching, and podcasts 24 hours a day since 2004 at
www.ancientfaith.com